2

CONTEMPORARY TOPICS

Academic Listening and Note-Taking Skills

THIRD EDITION

SCHOOL OF
ENGLISH

Ellen Kisslinger

Michael Rost
SERIES EDITOR

PEARSON
Longman

Contemporary Topics 2
High Intermediate
Academic Listening and Note-Taking Skills
Third Edition

Pearson Education, 10 Bank Street, White Plains, NY 10606

Staff credits: The people who made up the **Contemporary Topics 2** team, representing editorial, production, design, and manufacturing, are Rhea Banker, Danielle Belfiore, Dave Dickey, Christine Edmonds, Nancy Flaggman, Dana Klinek, Amy McCormick, Linda Moser, Carlos Rountree, Jennifer Stem, Leigh Stolle, Paula Van Ells, Kenneth Volcjak, and Pat Wosczyk.
Cover design: Rhea Banker
Cover art: © Jennifer Bartlett, Detail of *Rhapsody*. Photo: Geoffrey Clements/Corbis
Text composition: Integra Software Services, Pvt. Ltd.
Text font: Times 11.5/13
Credits: See page 133.

Library of Congress Cataloging-in-Publication Data
Kisslinger, Ellen.
Contemporary topics 2 : academic listening and note-taking skills / Ellen Kisslinger.—3rd ed.
    p. cm.
ISBN-13: 978-0-13-234524-8 (pbk.)
ISBN-10: 0-13-234524-2 (pbk.)
1. English language—Textbooks for foreign speakers. 2. English language—Spoken English.
3. Listening. 4. Listening comprehension. I. Title. II. Title: Contemporary topics two.
III. Title: Academic listening and note-taking skills.
PE1128.K4947 2009
428.3'4—dc22

2008039710

PEARSON LONGMAN ON THE **WEB**

Pearsonlongman.com offers online resources for teachers and students. Access our Companion Websites, our online catalog, and our local offices around the world.

Visit us at **www.pearsonlongman.com.**

Printed in the United States of America
5 6 7 8 9 10—V042—13 12 11 10

CONTENTS

SCOPE *and* sequence

UNIT SUBJECT AND TITLE	CORPUS-BASED VOCABULARY		NOTE-TAKING AND LISTENING FOCUS	DISCUSSION STRATEGIES	PROJECT
1 **SOCIOLOGY** **Names**	assignments classic discrimination gender	generations image prime symbol	Main ideas	■ Asking for opinions or ideas ■ Asking for clarification or confirmation	Research and present on name changes
2 **LINGUISTICS** **Global English**	acknowledge communicate domains facilitate global	nevertheless retained unprecedented	Comparisons	■ Agreeing ■ Disagreeing	Research and present on varieties of English
3 **PSYCHOLOGY** **Phobias**	constant duration physical	psychologist rational	Key words	■ Offering a fact or example ■ Asking for clarification or confirmation ■ Keeping the discussion on topic	Research and present on common or unusual phobias
4 **CULINARY ARTS** **Owning a Successful Restaurant**	components contrast contribute to emphasized	guarantee perspective	Topics and subtopics	■ Agreeing ■ Asking for clarification or confirmation ■ Paraphrasing	Research and present on food professions
5 **EDUCATION** **How We Each Learn Best**	accurately assess aware demonstrated	logic mental notion options	Numbered lists	■ Expressing an opinion ■ Offering a fact or example ■ Asking for clarification or confirmation	Research and present on what intelligences are valued in different cultures
6 **HISTORY** **The Silk Road**	alternate conflict decade	decline network route	Dates and numbers	■ Asking for opinions or ideas ■ Offering a fact or example ■ Asking for clarification or confirmation	Research and present on cultural impacts of the Silk Road

UNIT SUBJECT AND TITLE	CORPUS-BASED VOCABULARY		NOTE-TAKING AND LISTENING FOCUS	DISCUSSION STRATEGIES	PROJECT
7 **BUSINESS** **Team Building**	challenge enhance	project resolve sufficient summary	Symbols and abbreviations	■ Disagreeing ■ Keeping the discussion on topic ■ Trying to reach a consensus	Research and present on an existing company's culture
8 **ARCHITECTURE** **Frank Gehry**	dynamic foundation objective	principle stress utilize	Emphasis	■ Asking for opinions or ideas ■ Agreeing ■ Disagreeing	Research and present on topics in architecture
9 **PUBLIC HEALTH** **Building Immunity**	adapting to crucial exposed to incidence of microorganisms	promote recover resist stress transmitted	Connected ideas	■ Asking for opinions or ideas ■ Offering a fact or example ■ Paraphrasing	Research and present on tips for traveling abroad or jobs in public health
10 **MEDIA STUDIES** **Principles of Journalism**	adequately compiled covered ethics	objective paradigm professional underlying	Lecture organization	■ Expressing an opinion ■ Agreeing ■ Paraphrasing	Research and present on how news stories are reported or on community websites
11 **BIOLOGY** **DNA Testing**	access to concentrated on extract identical	medical reveal statistically	Graphic organizers	■ Expressing an opinion ■ Disagreeing ■ Keeping the discussion on topic	Research and present on various uses of DNA testing
12 **PUBLIC ADMINISTRATION** **Risk Management**	allocate cooperate ignore minimize mitigating predict	priorities targeted ultimately widespread	Questions	■ Asking for opinions or ideas ■ Agreeing ■ Offering a fact or example	Research and present on disaster survivors or relief organizations

ACKNOWLEDGMENTS

The series editor, authors, and publisher would like to thank the following consultants, reviewers, and teachers for offering their invaluable insights and suggestions for the third edition of the *Contemporary Topics* series.

Kate Reynolds, *University of Wisconsin-Eau Claire*; Kathie Gerecke, *North Shore Community College*; Jeanne Dunnett, *Central Connecticut State University*; Linda Anderson, *Washington University in St. Louis/Fontbonne University*; Sande Wu, *California State University, Fresno*; Stephanie Landon, *College of the Desert*; Jungsook Kim, *Jeungsang Language School*; Jenny Oh Kim, *Kangnamgu Daechidong*; Stephanie Landon, *Bunker Hill Community College*; Kathie Gerecke, *North Shore Community College*; Patty Heiser, *University of Washington*; Carrie Barnard, *Queens College*; Lori D. Giles, *University of Miami*; Sande Wu, *California State University, Fresno*; Kate Reynolds, *University of Wisconsin-Eau Claire*; Nancy H. Centers, *Roger Williams University*; Lyra Riabov, *Southern New Hampshire University*; Jeanne Dunnett, *Central Connecticut State University*; Dr. Steven Gras, *ESL Program, SUNY Plattsburgh*; series consultants Jeanette Clement and Cynthia Lennox, *Duquesne University*

The author would also like to thank Jennifer Bixby and Elly Schottman, as well as the many people at Pearson Education, in particular Amy McCormick and Leigh Stolle for their valuable support and dedication to the success of the series. I would also like to thank Michael Rost, with whom I've shared the challenge of addressing the needs of our students in academic listening for many years. His keen insight regarding the complexity of skills needed by students to support their success academically has made the series possible.

INTRODUCTION

Content-based learning is an exciting and effective way for students to acquire English. The *Contemporary Topics* series provides a fresh content-based approach that helps students develop their listening, note-taking, and discussion skills while studying interesting, relevant topics.

The *Contemporary Topics* series appeals to students in many different contexts because it utilizes a variety of multimedia technologies and caters to a range of learning styles. The *Contemporary Topics* series is ideal for students who are preparing to study in an English-speaking academic environment. It's also suitable for all students who simply wish to experience the richness of a content-based approach.

Each unit centers around a short academic lecture. Realistic preparation activities, focused listening tasks, personalized discussions, challenging tests, and authentic projects enable students to explore each topic deeply.

The lecture topics are drawn from a range of academic disciplines, feature engaging instructors with live student audiences, and take place in authentic lecture hall settings. The multimodal design of each lecture allows for various learning formats, including video- and audio-only presentations, optional text subtitling, optional Presentation Points slide support, and for DVD users, optional pop-up Coaching Tips.

In order to achieve the goals of content-based instruction, the *Contemporary Topics* series has developed an engaging eight-step learning methodology:

STEP 1: CONNECT *to the* topic   *Estimated Time: 10 minutes*

This opening section invites students to activate what they already know about the unit topic by connecting the topic to their personal experiences and beliefs. Typically, students fill out a short survey and compare answers with a partner. The teacher then acts as a facilitator for students to share some of their initial ideas about the topic before they explore it further.

STEP 2: BUILD *your* vocabulary   *Estimated Time: 15 minutes*

This section familiarizes students with some of the key content words and phrases used in the lecture. Each lecture contains 10–15 key words from the Academic Word List to ensure that students are exposed to the core vocabulary needed for academic success.

Students read and *listen to* target words and phrases in context, so that they can better prepare for the upcoming lecture. Students then work individually or with a partner to complete exercises to ensure an initial understanding of the target lexis of the unit. A supplementary Interact with Vocabulary! activity enables students to focus on form as they are learning new words and collocations.

STEP 3: F O C U S *your* attention   *Estimated Time: 10 minutes*

In this section, students learn strategies for listening actively and taking clear notes. Because a major part of "active listening" involves a readiness to deal with comprehension difficulties, this section provides specific tips to help students direct their attention and gain more control of how they listen.

Tips include using signal words as organization cues, making lists, noting definitions, linking examples to main ideas, identifying causes and effects, and separating points of view. A Try It Out! section, based on a short audio extract, allows students to work on listening and note-taking strategies before they get to the main lecture. Examples of actual notes are also provided in this section to give students concrete "starter models" they can use in the classroom.

STEP 4: L I S T E N *to the* lecture   *Estimated Time: 20–30 minutes*

As the central section of each unit, Listen to the Lecture allows for two full listening cycles, one to focus on "top-down listening" strategies (Listen for Main Ideas) and one to focus on "bottom-up listening" strategies (Listen for Details).

In keeping with the principles of content-based instruction, students are provided with several layers of support. In the Before You Listen section, students are guided to activate concepts and vocabulary they have studied earlier in the unit.

The lecture can be viewed in video mode or listened to in audio mode. In video mode, the lecture includes the speaker's Presentation Points and subtitles, for reinforcing comprehension (recommended as a final review). It also includes Coaching Tips on strategies for listening, note-taking, and critical thinking.

STEP 5: T A L K *about the* topic   *Estimated Time: 15 minutes*

Here students gain valuable discussion skills as they talk about the content of the lectures. Discussion skills are an important part of academic success, and most students benefit from structured practice with these skills. In this activity, students first listen to a short "model discussion" involving native and non-native speakers, and identify the speaking strategies and gambits that are used. They then attempt to use some of those strategies in their own discussion groups.

The discussion strategies modeled and explained across the twelve units include asking for and sharing opinions and ideas, agreeing and disagreeing, offering facts and examples, asking clarification questions, seeking confirmation, paraphrasing, and managing the discussion.

STEP 6: R E V I E W *your* notes   *Estimated Time: 15 minutes*

Using notes for review and discussion is an important study skill that is developed in this section. Research has shown that the value of note-taking for memory building is realized *primarily* when note-takers review their notes and attempt to reconstruct the content.

In this activity, students are guided in reviewing the content of the unit, clarifying concepts, and preparing for the Unit Test. Abbreviated examples of actual notes are provided to help students compare and improve their own note-taking skills.

STEP 7: TAKE *the unit* test *Estimated Time: 15 minutes*

This activity, Take the Unit Test, completes the study cycle of the unit: preparation for the lecture, listening to the lecture, review of the content, and assessment.

The Unit Test, contained only in the Teacher's Pack, is photocopied and distributed by the teacher, then completed in class, using the accompanying audio CDs. The tests in *Contemporary Topics* are intended to be challenging—to motivate students to learn the material thoroughly. The format features an answer sheet with choices. The question "stem" is provided on audio only.

Test-taking skills include verbatim recall, paraphrasing, inferencing, and synthesizing information from different parts of the lecture.

STEP 8: EXTEND *the* topic *Estimated time: 20 minutes minimum*

This final section creates a natural extension of the unit topic to areas that are relevant to students. Students first listen to a supplementary media clip drawn from a variety of interesting genres. Typically, students then choose an optional extension activity and prepare a class presentation.

By completing these eight steps, students gain valuable study skills to help them become confident and independent learners. The *Contemporary Topics* learning methodology and supporting multi-media package help students to develop stronger listening, speaking, and note-taking skills and strategies.

A supplementary **Teacher's Pack** (TP) contains Teaching Tips, transcripts, answer keys, and tests. The transcripts include the lectures, the student discussions, the test questions, and audio clips from Focus Your Attention and Extend the Topic. Full transcriptions of the DVD Coaching Tips and Presentation Points are available online at:

www.pearsonlongman.com/contemporarytopics

We hope you will enjoy using this course. While the *Contemporary Topics* series provides an abundance of learning activities and media, the key to making the course work in your classroom is student engagement and commitment. For content-based learning to be effective, students need to become *active* learners. This involves thinking critically, guessing, interacting, offering ideas, collaborating, questioning, and responding. The authors and editors of *Contemporary Topics* have created a rich framework for encouraging students to become active, successful learners. We hope that we have also provided you, the teacher, with tools for becoming an active guide to the students in their learning.

Michael Rost
Series Editor

TO *the* student

The goal of *Contemporary Topics* is to help you develop the skills and strategies you need to successfully participate in academic lectures. You will learn strategies for listening actively and taking clear notes. Good listening skills will help you follow lectures more easily, and good note-taking skills will help you better organize and understand—and later review—the information you've heard. As you use the book, you can develop a style of note-taking that works best for you.

Discussion skills are also an important part of academic success. You will have many opportunities to develop your speaking skills as you review lecture notes with a partner, as well as in other discussion activities where you can share ideas, reactions, and personal interests with your classmates.

Another key to academic success is building your vocabulary. Each unit familiarizes you with key words from the lecture, many of which are frequently used in academic situations. This ensures that you learn vocabulary that will be useful to you regardless of what major you decide on later.

By completing *Contemporary Topics,* you can feel confident that you'll be better prepared for academic work. Also, I encourage you to use the book as a starting point to explore on your own topics that interest you. Go online or use other resources to find out more. Share what you learn with your classmates. By doing research on your own, you will not only be more actively involved in the class, you will help yourself develop the academic skills you need to succeed in other classes in the future. I hope you enjoy using *Contemporary Topics.*

SOCIOLOGY

Names

Elton John's birth name was Reginald Dwight. Tiger Woods's actual first name is Eldrick.
And Queen Latifah was born Dana Owens.

CONNECT *to the* topic

Names are what we call a cultural universal. This means that all people have names regardless of their culture. And people respond differently to different names. Some people say that choosing a child's name is a major responsibility. Would you name your baby Candy Stohr, Mary Christmas, or Garage Empty? Some people have! How important is a name to you?

Take this survey about names. Read each statement. Then check (☑) your response.

	Agree	Disagree
My name makes me special.	_____	_____
My name doesn't matter. People can call me anything.	_____	_____
I would change my name to help my career.	_____	_____
My name is part of my identity.	_____	_____
The meaning of my name is very important to me.	_____	_____
Parents should be able to choose any name they want for their child.	_____	_____

Compare responses with a partner. Give reasons.

BUILD *your* vocabulary

A. **The boldfaced words are from this unit's lecture on names. Listen to each sentence. Then guess the meaning of the boldfaced word.**

1. Some parents **admire** famous athletes as strong role models, so they name their children after them.

2. Taylor had so many homework **assignments** that she had no time to watch TV.

3. A **classic** name is one that was popular years ago and is still common today.

4. In some families, it's the **custom** to give the firstborn boy the same name as his father and add "Junior."

5. Some parents are concerned about **discrimination**. They don't want their children treated unfairly because of their names.

6. A name like Hunter is **gender** neutral; it can be used for a boy or girl.

7. Women in three **generations** of my family have had the name Sarah—my grandmother, my mother, and my sister.

8. When I hear the name Barbie, I see an **image** of a tall, blond girl. Fair or not, it's the picture that comes into my mind.

9. John is a **prime** example of a classic name. It's been used for many years.

10. A name can be a **symbol** of identity, especially for celebrities.

B. **Now complete each sentence with the correct word.**

admire	classic	discrimination	generations	prime
assignments	custom	gender	image	symbol

1. A _____ name like Robert has been used for a long time.

2. Some people might say the name Tiger Woods is a(n) _____ of Tiger Woods's identity as a strong golfer.

3. The couple didn't want to know the _____ of their baby before it was born. Either a boy or a girl was fine.

4. In my opinion, a(n) _____ example of a bad name is a name that's hard to pronounce.

5. Mr. Lee gave his students three _____ for the weekend.

6. Because the Martins were worried about gender _____, they gave their daughter a name used by both boys and girls.

7. The _____ in our family is to name a baby after a relative who has recently died.

8. Luis forgot the woman's name although the _____ of her face was easy to remember.

9. In Robert's family, four _____ have the name "Robert," including Robert's great-grandfather.

10. For their new baby, my neighbors chose the name of a politician they _____ in hopes that their daughter will also be successful.

C. *INTERACT WITH VOCABULARY!* **Read the sentences with a partner. Notice the boldfaced words. Then choose a particle to complete each sentence.**

after	as	by	of	to

1. An **example** _____ an unusual name is Sky.

2. Unfortunately, people are **judged** _____ the names they have.

3. Stephen was **named** _____ his dad's college coach, Mr. Stevens.

4. Emily **qualifies** _____ a classic name because it's always been popular.

5. Sociologists study how people **respond** _____ each other.

down	on	out of	to	with

6. Stereotypes are **associated** _____ some names. For example, some people expect a Jennifer to be pretty.

7. Some couples choose a name in hopes it'll provide some social **benefit** _____ their child.

8. The name Anna was **passed** _____ from one generation to the next in the girl's family.

9. Some parents don't **rely** _____ custom. Instead, they choose a name they like.

10. A classic name never goes _____ **style**. It's always popular.

FOCUS *your* attention

MAIN IDEAS

There are two basic reasons for taking lecture notes:

- to help you focus on the **main ideas** of a lecture
- to help you review the information later

A speaker usually introduces main ideas with **signal phrases**. For example:

> **In the first half,** you'll hear about . . .
>
> **In the second half,** we'll discuss . . .
>
> Today's lecture **will focus on** . . .
>
> This afternoon **we'll look at** . . .
>
> **I'd like to begin with** the first category . . .
>
> Today's lecture will be **divided into two parts** . . .

Paying attention to the introduction can help you organize your notes. For example:

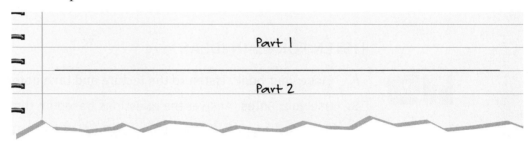

Part 1

Part 2

TRY
IT
OUT!

A. **Listen to this excerpt from a sociology lecture. What signal phrases do you hear? What two topics will the lecturer be discussing? Take notes.**

B. **Compare notes with a partner. Use your notes to answer these questions.**

LISTEN *to the* lecture

BEFORE YOU LISTEN

You are about to listen to this unit's lecture on names. Think of two common ways parents choose names.

_____

_____

LISTEN FOR MAIN IDEAS

A. **Close your book. Listen to the lecture and take notes.**

B. **Use your notes. Answer the questions based on the lecture. Circle *a*, *b*, or *c*.**

1. What does calling the speaker "Alex" versus "Dr. Shaw" show?

   a. how names can influence how we respond to people

   b. how we can change our names

   c. which name the speaker prefers students use with her

2. What is the most common way parents choose a name?

   a. They follow family customs.

   b. They choose what's popular.

   c. They choose a name they like.

3. How is a classic name defined?

   a. as a name that has a good sound

   b. as a name that doesn't go out of style

   c. as a name that has a nice feeling

4. Does an unusual name make someone successful?

    a. Yes, the research shows this.

    b. Yes, sociologists agree on this.

    c. No, the research doesn't show this.

5. What does the example about the names Michael and Hubert tell us?

    a. that there are stereotypes associated with names

    b. that Michael is a classic name

    c. that other people aren't affected by our names

LISTEN FOR DETAILS

A. Close your book. Listen to the lecture again. Add details to your notes and correct any mistakes.

B. Use your notes. Decide if the sentences below are *T* (true) or *F* (false), according to the lecture. Correct the false statements.

____ 1. A cultural universal is defined as a practice we all share.

____ 2. A first name is also referred to as a given name.

____ 3. In some families, it's custom to name the first son after the grandmother.

____ 4. Taylor is an example of a name that works for either gender.

____ 5. Some parents believe a name can give their child social benefit.

____ 6. Alex and Emily are examples of classic names.

____ 7. Sociologists don't know if it's better to have a classic or an unusual name.

____ 8. The name Hubert was on all of the homework assignments.

____ 9. The teachers were given the same homework assignment.

____ 10. Parents who want their son to be considered smart should name him Hubert.

TALK *about the* topic

A. **Listen to the students talk about names. Read each comment. Then check (☑) the student who makes the comment.**

		Mia	Manny	Hannah	River
1.	"(My name) was just a name my parents liked. Pretty simple!"	☐	☐	☐	☐
2.	"In my case, I got my name from the first way that the lecturer mentioned, which was custom."	☐	☐	☐	☐
3.	"I was named after my mom's high school teacher. I guess my mom really admired this woman."	☐	☐	☐	☐
4.	"I'm not really sure where my name comes from. I doubt my parents chose it to help me socially."	☐	☐	☐	☐

Mia

Manny

Hannah

River

B. **Listen to the discussion again. Listen closely for the comments below. Check (☑) the discussion strategy the student uses.**

		Asking for opinions or ideas	Asking for clarification or confirmation
1.	**Mia:** "So you must think names really do matter?"	☐	☐
2.	**Hannah:** "This lecture's made me realize it's a big responsibility for a parent to choose ... Don't you think?"	☐	☐
3.	**Mia:** "You mean, it's the parents' responsibility to give good names?"	☐	☐

> **Discussion Strategy:** To **clarify** means to make clearer. To **confirm** is to remove doubt. You can clarify or confirm by restating what you understood: "You mean . . . " or ask "Do you mean . . . ?" Or you can ask open-ended questions like "What do you mean?" and "Could you clarify . . . ?"

C. **In small groups, discuss one or more of these topics. Try to use the discussion strategies you have learned.**

- Do you know people with unusual names? How has it affected them?
- In your experience, are stereotypes associated with names? Give examples.
- There are many baby name websites. Is this a good way to choose a name?

REVIEW *your* notes

Work with a partner. Use your notes. Take turns explaining the main ideas from the lecture. Then complete the notes below.

Name:	Ex. of:
Alex / Alexandra / Dr. Shaw	how different names change what we think of people
Sarah	
Robert or Anna	
Darvlin	
Taylor	
Hubert	

Now you are ready to take the Unit Test.

TAKE THE UNIT TEST

> **Tip!**
>
> Remember: There are two basic reasons for taking notes:
> - to help you focus on the main ideas of a lecture
> - to help you later review information

EXTEND *the* topic

Now that you've learned more about the sociology of names, think about the question you considered at the beginning of this unit: How important is a name to you? Expand your understanding of names with the following activities.

A. Listen to a student radio reporter interview a student for a feature about names. Then discuss these questions with your classmates.

1. There are trends in names. Some names are very popular, and then go out of style. What are some disadvantages of naming a baby a trendy name, like Auriel?

2. What names are trendy now?

B. Read these comments from parents.

How we named our baby ...

We searched baby name databases online for hours, reading the meanings of names. We considered David, which means beloved; Robert, which means bright flame; and Skylar, which means scholar. We

went with Skylar. It's a nice name, and a scholar in the family would be good!

My husband and I decided we needed to choose a name that was in harmony with the date and year our daughter was born. We met with an astrologist who told us what to name her. She told us to call her Eliza.

For us, it was easy. One of the characters on our favorite TV show had a baby boy. So, we named our son the same name! Why not? We like the name Ramon. Who knows? Maybe our son'll be on TV, too, someday.

My wife and I wanted a name that sounded pleasing and created a positive feeling, so we read names aloud. We asked ourselves: Does this name have a nice sound? Does it go with our last name? For us, the sound had to be just right. So, we named our daughter Sophie.

Which of these methods do you agree with? Discuss with a partner.

Musician Louis Armstrong was nicknamed Satchmo—short for "satchel (a small bag) mouth."
Mary Ann Evans is better known as George Eliot, the pen name she wrote under.

C. Research names. Prepare a five-minute presentation on one of these topics.

┈┈┈> Many celebrities, such as Elton John and Queen Latifah, have changed
their names. Think of other celebrities who have interesting names. Are
those their original names? Find examples of three other celebrities who
changed their names. Why do you think they did it?

┈┈┈> There are many websites with tips for choosing names. Go to several
sites. Compare tips. Take brief notes on three important tips the
websites all mention.

UNIT 2

Global English

CONNECT *to the* topic

Most people would agree that English is the current lingua franca *of the world—that is, the most commonly used language. On the Internet and in face-to-face situations—at airports, hotels, and business meetings—English is the international language of choice. And, as the global economy continues to grow, more people than ever before will be studying English.*

Answer these questions about using English.

⋯⋯> In what situations do you use English now?

⋯⋯> Do you use American slang?

⋯⋯> In what future situations might you need English?

⋯⋯> What jobs in your country require English?

⋯⋯> How often do you speak English with someone whose first language is not English?

⋯⋯> Why do you think English has become the common language of the world?

Compare responses with a partner.

BUILD *your* vocabulary

A. The boldfaced words are from this unit's lecture on English as a global language. Listen to each sentence. Then guess the meaning of the boldfaced word.

1. Most people **acknowledge** that English is used all over the world. There is very little disagreement about that.

2. In many international situations, people **communicate** in English.

3. English is used widely in certain **domains**, such as business and science.

4. The Portuguese taxi driver and the German tourist used English to **facilitate** communication because it was the only language they both knew.

5. English is considered a **global** language because it's used on every continent.

6. Many people in Japan can speak some English. **Nevertheless**, this doesn't mean English is their primary language; Japanese is.

7. English is one of the **official** languages of the European Union. It's used among EU representatives in major meetings.

8. Because the flight attendant was **proficient** in English, French, and Spanish, he could speak with almost all of the passengers.

9. The hotel employees in Beijing learned English, but, of course, **retained** their ability to speak Chinese. Now they use both languages at work.

10. The number of people who currently speak some English is **unprecedented**. More people speak it now than ever before.

B. Now circle the best definition for each boldfaced word.

1. Most people **acknowledge** …

   wish   prefer   accept as true

2. the language used to **communicate** in

   share information   call   present

3. used in certain **domains**

   organizations   areas or fields   factors

4. to **facilitate** communication

   present   slow down   help make happen

5. a **global** language

   important   worldwide   large

6. **Nevertheless**, this doesn't mean …

   although true   in addition   furthermore

7. one of the **official** languages

   correct   informal   approved by an authority

8. **proficient** in both English and Spanish

   productive   skillful   creative

9. **retained** their ability

   kept   refused   lost

10. the number of people is **unprecedented**

    unknown   unnoticed   never happened before

C. *INTERACT WITH VOCABULARY!* **Work in pairs. Take turns saying the sentences, ordering the words correctly.**

1. The linguistics professor (an / **authority** / is / **on**) the use of English.

2. In the future, (English / **of** / used / be / will / **instead**) other languages like French and Chinese?

3. I know that there are (**view / points** / contrasting / two / **of**) about English.

4. Thomas grew up speaking English but (languages / **proficient** / was / four / **in** / other) as well.

5. The idea (is / linguists / **by** / **supported** / many) and is popular.

6. Some contend that other languages won't (be / **replaced** / English / **by**).

7. It's evident that (use / **work** / English / many / **at** / people), but not at home.

8. Will non-English-speaking countries (**hold** / **to** / want / **on** / to) their own languages?

9. I don't believe (an / need / we / that / **standard** / **international**) for English.

10. Some people, like taxi drivers, may only know (**for** / English / the / **required**) their jobs.

FOCUS *your* attention

COMPARISONS

At the beginning of a lecture that compares ideas, a speaker often will say how the lecture is going to be organized. For example:

> Today you'll hear **two contrasting points of view** about learning English.
>
> This afternoon we'll **compare** American English and British English.
>
> We'll look at some of **the differences between** written and spoken English.

When you hear these signal words, one way to organize your notes is to use two columns to separate the ideas you hear. Say you hear *Today I'm going to present two contrasting points of view about varieties of English: One view is that it's a problem; the other view is that it isn't.* Your notes might look like this:

Varieties of English: A Problem?

A problem	Not a problem
1.	1.
2.	2.
3.	3.

TRY IT OUT!

A. Listen to this excerpt from a talk about varieties of English. What ideas do you hear? Take notes.

B. Compare notes with a partner.

LISTEN *to the* lecture

In India, English is one of the most widely spoken languages.

BEFORE YOU LISTEN

You are about to listen to this unit's lecture on English as a global language. Do you think English will continue to be the world's *lingua franca*? Give two reasons for your answer.

_____

LISTEN FOR MAIN IDEAS

A. **Close your book. Listen to the lecture and take notes.**

B. **Use your notes. Answer the questions based on the lecture. Circle *a*, *b*, or *c*.**

1. What aspect of English as a global language does the speaker mainly discuss?

   a. why people like to use English

   b. whether English will eventually replace other languages

   c. where English is most popular

2. What is the main reason given for the widespread use of English?

   a. There are many Internet users.

   b. There is a need for a common language.

   c. English speakers want everyone to learn English.

3. Why does the speaker mention that English is the dominant language of science and international business?

   a. to show that scientists like English

   b. to show that a common language is necessary

   c. to show that people prefer other languages

4. Why is English not considered a truly global language by some people?

    a. because many people are now proficient in English

    b. because many people don't use it for primary communication at home

    c. because many people are studying English now

5. What is the speaker's view of English as a global language?

    a. that it will continue to be the *lingua franca*, but not replace other languages

    b. that it will continue to be the *lingua franca*, and replace other languages

    c. that it will not continue to be the *lingua franca* because there are too many varieties

LISTEN FOR DETAILS

A. **Close your book. Listen to the lecture again. Add details to your notes and correct any mistakes.**

B. **Use your notes. Decide if the statements below are *T* (true) or *F* (false), according to the lecture. Correct the false statements.**

_____ 1. Professor Kachru called the current use of English "unprecedented."

_____ 2. The first point of view presented is that English won't replace other languages.

_____ 3. The other point of view is that, internationally, English is the main language in people's daily lives.

_____ 4. Business schools in France are now fighting hard to keep English out.

_____ 5. More than a billion people speak English as their first language.

_____ 6. India is mentioned as a country where English is an official language.

_____ 7. Most Korean pilots speak English at home instead of Korean.

_____ 8. Currently, seventy-five countries use English as an official language.

_____ 9. The speaker supports David Crystal's point of view of English as a global language.

_____ 10. The speaker says there must be an international standard for English.

TALK *about the* topic

A. Listen to the students talk about English as a global language. Read each comment. Then check (✓) the student who makes the comment.

	Michael	May	Yhinny	Qiang
1. "You know when the lecturer was talking about languages and culture?"	☐	☐	☐	☐
2. "I need English for class now, or maybe someday at my job."	☐	☐	☐	☐
3. "What about the idea of having an international standard for English?"	☐	☐	☐	☐
4. "It's like a set of rules for grammar, spelling … that everyone agrees to."	☐	☐	☐	☐

B. Listen to the discussion again. Listen closely for the comments below. Check (✓) the discussion strategy the student uses.

	Agreeing	Disagreeing
1. **May:** "Oh, definitely."	☐	☐
2. **Qiang:** "Right! I don't see other languages disappearing."	☐	☐
3. **May:** "Oh, it's the same with me."	☐	☐
4. **May:** "You're joking, right?"	☐	☐

Discussion Strategy: In most conversations, **expressing disagreement** without seeming to be too disagreeable is key! One way to do so is to first acknowledge the other person's point: "I see what you're saying, but . . . " Or you can be direct: "I simply disagree." Some people like to soften their position with an apology: "I'm sorry, but . . . " And of course, body language and tone can further "shape" your message.

C. In small groups, discuss one or more of these topics. Try to use the discussion strategies you have learned.

- Why do you think English has become the common language for globalization?
- Do you agree that as more people learn English, their desire to hold on to their own cultures will get stronger?
- If you were to establish an international standard for English, what would the rules be for grammar? Vocabulary? Pronunciation?

REVIEW *your* notes

Paraphrase means to retell something in your own words. Work with a partner. Take turns paraphrasing the main ideas from the lecture. Then use your notes to complete the outline below.

I.   Def. of a global language:

II. 1st point of view:

     A. Support:
     B. Support:
     C. Support:

III. Contrasting point of view:

     A. Support:
     B. Support:
     C. Support:

IV. Conclusions:

     A. About the future of English? Other languages?

     B. About the need for an international standard?

TAKE THE UNIT TEST

Now you are ready to take the Unit Test.

Tip!

Remember: Focus on the **similarities** and **differences** between ideas.

EXTEND *the* topic

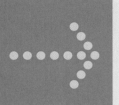

What have you learned about English that you didn't know before? Has it impacted your feelings about studying English? The following listening, reading, and research activities are a chance to enhance your understanding of English as a global language.

A. **Listen to a speaker present at an international forum on languages. Discuss these questions with your classmates.**

1. How did you decide which variety of English to study?

2. How important is pronunciation to you? Have you experienced any problems because of pronunciation?

B. **Read about an area where the use of English is growing.**

After finishing her undergraduate studies in Italy, Antonia Francesco began her search for a graduate business program. She considered dozens of programs around the world. Ultimately, she chose Essec, a top business school near Paris where now nearly half of the courses are taught in English. This, Antonia knew, meant not only a program with a global business focus, but also an international mix of students and the chance to improve her English.

Essec isn't alone in its push to teach required classes in English. Many of the world's top business schools and universities are now doing this. Schools know English is the *lingua franca* of the global economy. Teaching courses in English prepares their students to use English in the global job market. It also attracts international students like Antonia as well as students from English-speaking countries. In their classes, students experience using English as their common language—a skill they'll need no matter where they work later on.

Discuss these questions with a partner.

---> Have you taken any university courses taught in English in your home country?

---> Is it fair for students from non-English-speaking countries like France to be required to take courses taught in English? What are some advantages and disadvantages?

C.   Research varieties of English.

Some words have different meanings depending on the variety of English they come from. For example, in the United States, a *bonnet* is a type of hat; whereas in England, a *bonnet* is a part of a car. Other examples include *truck* (U.S.) versus *lorry* (U.K.) and *elevator* (U.S.) versus *lift* (U.K.).

Follow these steps.

1.   Research other varieties of English, such as South African, Indian, Australian, or Singaporean English. Think about the English used in your own country as well.

2.   Find examples of at least three pairs of words or phrases that have different meanings depending on the variety of English.

3.   Prepare a presentation for the class or small group.

UNIT 3

Phobias

CONNECT *to the* topic

Are you afraid of anything? Of course you are—we all are! It's natural to be afraid of things we think could harm us. But some fears aren't normal. These are called phobias. *A* phobia *is a very strong, unreasonable fear. Common phobias include* acrophobia, *a fear of heights, and* arachnophobia, *a fear of spiders.*

Read these statements about fears and phobias. Then check (☑) your response.

	Agree	Disagree
Fear can help us to survive real dangers.	____	____
Our culture teaches us what to be afraid of.	____	____
A fear of fire or a big storm is a normal fear.	____	____
Most people are afraid of trying new things.	____	____
Fear can keep us from doing what we say we want to do.	____	____
Medication seems like the best way to treat a phobia.	____	____
People with phobias are actually afraid of something deeper.	____	____
If you have a phobia, it's better to tell someone than to hide it.	____	____

Compare responses with a partner.

BUILD *your* vocabulary

A. The boldfaced words are from this unit's lecture on phobias. Listen to each sentence. Then guess the meaning of the boldfaced word.

1. Mark studied psychology because he was interested in human **behavior**.

2. Shaking is a common **characteristic** of a scared person.

3. Phobias are **classified** into categories including specific fears, such as the fear of dogs, and situational fears, such as the fear of speaking in public.

4. My uncle's fear of public places was **constant**; he never left his house.

5. After seeing an airplane crash, Lydia **developed** aerophobia. She panicked when she even saw an airplane and never flew again.

6. The **duration** of his fear of water was short. After just a few weeks of swimming lessons, he was cured.

7. Jan's **physical** response to the dark was extreme. She would start shaking and sweating as soon as the lights went out.

8. A **psychologist** can help patients with phobias look for deeper problems.

9. Tara couldn't be **rational** when she saw a cat. She couldn't think clearly.

10. When Martin was a boy, he was in a serious car accident. This childhood **trauma** made him too afraid to drive.

B. Now circle the best definition for each boldfaced word.

1. human **behavior**

    actions   feelings   ideas

2. two common **characteristics**

    features   feelings   problems

3. **classified** into three categories

    grouped   dismissed   treated

4. His fear was **constant**.

    irregular   continuous   very slow

5. **developed** acrophobia

    removed   began to have   recovered from

6. The **duration** was short.

    size   length of time   distance

7. a **physical** response

    related to emotions   related to the body   related to feelings

8. The **psychologist** took care of the patient.

| instructor | sleep researcher | person who treats mental problems |

9. too afraid to be **rational**

| unreasonable | reasonable | emotional |

10. a childhood **trauma**

| interesting experience | fun experience | bad experience |

C. *INTERACT WITH VOCABULARY!* Work with a partner. Read the sentences in Column A and discuss the meanings of the boldfaced phrases. Then read sentences 1–5 aloud as your partner fills in the blanks in Column B. Switch roles for 6–10.

Column A	**Column B**
1. Phobias are **classified by** the thing that is feared.	1. Phobias are **classified** _____ the thing that is feared.
2. What's the **definition of** a phobia?	2. What's the **definition** _____ a phobia?
3. There are various **theories on** the causes of phobias.	3. There are various **theories** _____ the causes of phobias.
4. An interesting **topic in** psychology is phobias.	4. An interesting **topic** _____ psychology is phobias.
5. One **type of** phobias is situational phobias.	5. One **type** _____ phobias is situational phobias.
6. Tomas was injured by a cat and became **afraid of** them.	6. Tomas was injured by a cat and became **afraid** _____ them.
7. The child's **reaction to** the dark was to cry.	7. The child's **reaction** _____ the dark was to cry.
8. Some phobias tend to **run in families**.	8. Some phobias tend to **run** _____ **families**.
9. There is a variety of **treatments for** phobias.	9. There is a variety of **treatments** _____ phobias.
10. A phobia may be a **sign of** a deep psychological problem.	10. A phobia may be a **sign** _____ a deep psychological problem.

FOCUS *your* attention

KEY WORDS

Speakers use a variety of cues to let you know when they are about to focus on a key word in the lecture. They may give any of the following cues:

- Pause
- Slow down
- Speak more loudly
- Repeat the key word
- Spell the key word
- Define the key word using an introductory phrase. For example:
  One is called . . .
  One (example) is . . .
  The first (type) is . . .

One way to note key words is to write the key word on the left and the definition on the right. Say you hear *A phobia—that's p-h-o-b-i-a—is an extreme fear.* Your notes might look like this:

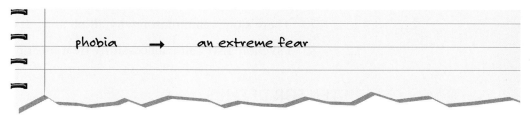

phobia → an extreme fear

TRY IT OUT!

A. Listen to this excerpt from a psychology lecture. Take notes below. What key word cues do you hear? What key words?

B. Compare notes and answers with a partner.

LISTEN *to the* lecture

BEFORE YOU LISTEN

You are about to listen to a psychology lecture on phobias. Why do you think some people develop phobias?

_____

LISTEN FOR MAIN IDEAS

A. **Close your book. Listen to the lecture and take notes.**

B. **Use your notes. According to the lecture, which of these statements are true? Make a check (✓).**

____ 1. A phobia doesn't interfere with someone's life.

____ 2. Phobias are extreme fears of a common object or situation.

____ 3. People with phobias often have strong physical reactions.

____ 4. The speaker discusses two types of phobias: specific and situational.

____ 5. Psychologists have defined the characteristics of a phobia.

____ 6. Phobias only run in families.

____ 7. There's one main reason why all phobias develop.

____ 8. Psychologists can't successfully treat most phobias.

LISTEN FOR DETAILS

A. **Close your book. Listen to the lecture again. Add details to your notes and correct any mistakes.**

B. **Use your notes. Choose the word or phrase that best completes each idea, based on the lecture.**

1. A phobia is a very strong, very _____ fear.

   a. weird

   b. focused

   c. personal

2. A phobia can often _____ a person's life.

   a. help

   b. strengthen

   c. interfere with

3. A phobia is not a(n) _____ response.

   a. necessary

   b. rational

   c. uncontrollable

4. A phobia will often _____ a long time.

   a. last

   b. develop over

   c. disappear after

5. A person with cynophobia will probably avoid _____.

   a. cats

   b. dogs

   c. open spaces

6. A boy develops a phobia by watching his father. This is an example of

   _____.

   a. direct learning

   b. association theory

   c. indirect learning

7. A woman fell into a lake when she was a child, and now she won't go
   near water. This example shows _____.

   a. indirect learning

   b. the association theory

   c. that phobias run in families

8. To treat a phobia, a psychologist tries to change the patient's

   _____.

   a. childhood trauma

   b. family situation

   c. behavior

TALK *about the* topic

A. Listen to the students talk about phobias. Read each comment. Then check (☑) the student who makes the comment.

		Alana	Ayman	Molly	Rob
1.	"I don't know if it's a phobia, but I hate spiders. I'm completely terrified of them."	☐	☐	☐	☐
2.	"Well, but those are natural reactions, don't you think?"	☐	☐	☐	☐
3.	"Un-control-able. So, something that you can't control."	☐	☐	☐	☐
4.	"Well, back home we don't believe in getting therapy for these kind(s) of problems."	☐	☐	☐	☐

B. Listen to the discussion again. Listen closely for the comments below. Check (☑) the discussion strategy the student uses.

		Offering a fact or example	Asking for clarification or confirmation	Keeping the discussion on topic
1.	**Ayman:** "Seriously guys . . . let's stay focused, OK?"	☐	☐	☐
2.	**Rob:** "I'm the same way with snakes. . . . I was hiking last summer . . . "	☐	☐	☐
3.	**Alana:** "Wait. What does that mean . . . ?"	☐	☐	☐
4.	**Ayman:** "That part of the definition made me think of my friend back in Dubai . . . "	☐	☐	☐

Discussion Strategy: In study groups or other organized conversations, **keeping the discussion on topic** is in everyone's best interest. While tangents (related topics) can be interesting, it's fair to remind others of the focus. Common expressions include "I'd like to get back to . . . ," "We're getting a little off track . . . ," and the very informal "Anyway!"

C. In small groups, discuss one or more of these topics. Try to use the discussion strategies you have learned.

- Suppose your friend was afraid of revolving doors. What could you do to help?
- Do you know anyone with a phobia? Describe the person's behavior.
- What are some "normal" fears that you, your friends, or family members have?

REVIEW *your* notes

Read your notes. Did you write down the key words and phrases from the lecture? Can you explain them? Work with a partner. Take turns explaining the ideas from the lecture. Then complete the notes below.

- Def. of a phobia:

- Main kinds of phobias:

1)

Ex.:

2)

Ex.:

- Characteristics of a phobia:

1)

2)

3)

- Classification system of phobias:

- Ex's of names of phobias:

- 2 theories on causes of phobias:

1)

2)

TAKE THE UNIT TEST

Now you are ready to take the Unit Test.

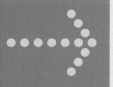# EXTEND *the* topic

> *Phobias are a fascinating psychological subject, but they are difficult conditions for those who struggle with them. Listen and read on to learn more about how phobias can impact people's lives—and how they can be treated.*

A. **Listen to a TV talk show guest share with the audience her experience with a phobia. Discuss these questions with your classmates.**

1. If you were Stephanie's doctor, what treatment would you suggest?

2. A fear of heights is fairly common. What other common phobias might interfere with a person's life?

B. **Read about three different approaches to treating phobias.**

Dr. Ella Simmons

I prescribe medicine right away. I have found that most patients first need medicine to calm down. Then, I can help them work on their phobias. In my view, the pharmaceutical approach is the quickest way to address phobias—and after years of suffering, patients welcome a quick answer.

Neil Lightfoot, PhD.

I prefer exposure therapy, or desensitization. I expose the patient to the phobic object or situation in steps. For example, if a patient is afraid of dogs, first I ask him or her to just think about dogs, then look at pictures of dogs, then look at live dogs, and eventually touch a dog. Gradually, the patient learns to not feel afraid. I find this treatment works well for many specific phobias.

Lauren Rose, M.A.

I'm a hypnotherapist. I play soft music. While the patient relaxes, I tell a story that helps the patient imagine being comfortable with whatever he or she is afraid of. Usually after a couple of sessions, the phobia is gone.

If you had a phobia, which treatment would you try? Discuss with a partner.

C. Research a common phobia—such as agoraphobia, the fear of public places—or an unusual phobia. Write a five-minute presentation based on the questions below. Present in groups. Compare information.

----> What are the characteristics of the phobia?

----> How common is it?

----> What treatments are used? What other treatments do you think might help?

For people with cynophobia, desensitization to dogs over several therapy sessions can cure the phobia.

UNIT 4

Owning a Successful Restaurant

What kind of eating experienced do you prefer? Casual, fast food, or fine dining?

CONNECT *to the* topic

Have you ever thought about being a restaurant owner? What kind of restaurant would you start? Many restaurants are not successful and go out of business in the first couple of years. What do you think is the key to success? Researchers often ask customers: What's important to you when you go to a restaurant? How would you answer?

Read how some customers responded.

> *Food: Fresh ingredients and interesting dishes*

> Comfort: Where I sit is very important.

> Price: Not too expensive

> Atmosphere: Good lighting and soft music

> Mood: A fun place to be

> *Service: I like waitstaff to pay attention to what I need.*

Work with a partner. Compare your responses with the customers'.

BUILD *your* vocabulary

A. The boldfaced words are from this unit's lecture on owning a successful restaurant. Listen to each sentence. Choose the meaning of the boldfaced word.

1. I felt relaxed by the café's **ambience**: the soft lighting, the quiet music, and the comfortable chairs.

   activity   atmosphere ✓   location

2. There are many expenses in running a restaurant. An owner needs to **balance** his or her desire to make money with the customers' desire for good prices.

   give equal importance to ✓   experiment with   exchange

3. Delicious food and comfortable tables are two **components** of a good dining experience.

   reasons ✓   parts   atmosphere

4. There was a big **contrast** between the two restaurants. One had great food; the other's was awful.

   increase   difference ✓   decrease

5. Good food and a talented waitstaff both **contribute to** a pleasant dining experience.

   help to reduce   help to make happen   help to avoid

6. The owner **emphasized** to the staff the importance of being on time. Otherwise, they'd be fired.

   guaranteed   obtained   stressed

7. A restaurant must be well organized. But it takes more than that to **guarantee** success—good food, for example, is also necessary.

   make certain   try   agree to

8. At first the chef seemed unfriendly, but the **opposite** was true. He was nice.

   something stronger   something less   something as
                                                   different as possible

9. At the **outset**, the waiter seemed skilled. But as the meal continued, his inexperience became clear.

   conclusion   concept   beginning

10. To be a successful restaurant owner, you must consider not only how you see things, but the customer's **perspective** as well.

    viewpoint   opinion   preferences

B. *INTERACT WITH VOCABULARY!* **Work with a partner. Read the sentences in Column A and discuss the meanings of the boldfaced phrases. Then read sentences 1–5 aloud as your partner fills in the blanks in Column B. Switch roles for 6–10.**

Column A	Column B
1. A good chef likes to **bring enjoyment to people** through food.	1. A good chef likes to **bring enjoyment** _____ **people** through food.
2. Every successful restaurant owner knows that a great dining experience is **built on** contrast.	2. Every successful restaurant owner knows that a great dining experience is **built** _____ contrast.
3. The restaurant owner wanted to **create for** her customers a special ambience.	3. The restaurant owner wanted to **create** _____ her customers a special ambience.
4. Let's consider one of the essential **factors in** a positive dining experience.	4. Let's consider one of the essential **factors** _____ a positive dining experience.
5. Andre made **a reservation for dinner** for 7 P.M. at his favorite French bistro, *Potager*.	5. Andre made **a reservation** _____ **dinner** for 7 P.M. at his favorite French bistro, *Potager*.
6. For their anniversary, the couple was **looking forward to** a romantic dinner.	6. For their anniversary, the couple was **looking forward** _____ a romantic dinner.
7. The customers were quite **satisfied with** the delicious food!	7. The customers were quite **satisfied** _____ the delicious food!
8. That Italian restaurant *Bello!* is **known for** its creative menu.	8. That Italian restaurant *Bello!* is **known** _____ its creative menu.
9. The **success of** a restaurant is based on many factors, starting with an owner with good business sense.	9. The **success** _____ a restaurant is based on many factors, starting with an owner with good business sense.
10. We were very **content with** our entire meal.	10. We were very **content** _____ our entire meal.

F O C U S *your* **attention**

TOPICS AND SUBTOPICS

In a lecture, there is usually one main topic and one or more subtopics. Subtopics are more specific subjects under the main topic. For example, if the main topic is restaurants, two subtopics might be fast-food restaurants and expensive, upscale restaurants. At the beginning of a lecture, a speaker often describes how the subtopics will be presented. Listen carefully to understand how the lecture will be organized. For example:

Today we're going to **talk about** *types of restaurants.* (main topic) **I want to focus first on** *fast-food restaurants.* (subtopic) **Then I plan to consider** *upscale restaurants.* (subtopic)

This afternoon I'm going to **discuss** *creating a menu.* (main topic) **Specifically, we'll look at two aspects:** *the design of the menu* (subtopic) *and what food categories to include.* (subtopic)

One way to take notes is to write the topic, and then indent the subtopics below. For example:

(topic) types of restaurants:
   (subtopic) fast-food restaurants
   (subtopic) upscale restaurants

TRY IT OUT!

A. Listen to this excerpt from a talk about one feature of a restaurant. Take notes. What is the main topic? What are the subtopics?

B. Compare notes with a partner. Use your notes to answer the questions.

LISTEN *to the* lecture

BEFORE YOU LISTEN

You are about to listen to a culinary arts lecture on running a successful restaurant. Many restaurants don't succeed. What do you think is the key to a restaurant's success?

_____

LISTEN FOR MAIN IDEAS

A. **Close your book. Listen to the lecture and take notes.**

B. **Use your notes. Answer the questions, based on the lecture. Circle *a*, *b*, or *c*.**

1. One of the speaker's main points is that _____.

   a. having a restaurant is enjoyable

   b. many factors contribute to success

   c. it's difficult to make customers happy

2. What does "a successful dining experience is built on contrast" mean?

   a. that the food should be good and the place fun

   b. that the place should be upscale but the food simple

   c. that the staff must work hard so that the customers can relax

3. Which of the following statements would the speaker agree with?

   a. A great chef guarantees a restaurant's success.

   b. The staff is really more important than the food.

   c. An owner must understand the restaurant as a business.

4. What is one of the most essential factors in a restaurant's success?

   a. the location

   b. the ambience

   c. the waitstaff

5. How should a restaurant "meet expectations"?

   a. by creating the ambience

   b. by taking care of the tables

   c. by doing everything customers want

6. What's the point of the speaker's brigade system explanation?

    a. to show how all the work gets done

    b. to show what the chef and cooks do

    c. to show how the tables are arranged

7. What made Kate and Justin's dinner a success?

    a. the fact that it was Kate's birthday

    b. the fact that Dante's understood what it needed to do

    c. the fact that Dante's was an upscale restaurant

LISTEN FOR DETAILS

A. Close your book. Listen to the lecture again. Add details to your notes and correct any mistakes.

B. Use your notes. Complete the sentences below, according to the lecture.

furniture	independent	lasts	rules	social

1. Only about one in five independent restaurants _____ more than five years.

2. About 50 percent of all restaurants are _____.

3. A restaurant owner must decide what kind of _____ experience to create.

4. The _____, the lighting, the music, and the staff's clothing all work together to create a restaurant's ambience.

5. The speaker says contrast _____ the restaurant business.

flowed	house	kitchen	menu	tables	typical

6. Justin and Kate are considered _____ customers because of their high expectations for Saturday night.

7. Dante's has a creative _____ with delicious choices.

8. In the brigade system, _____ means restaurant.

9. The brigade in the front takes care of the _____, while the brigade in the back takes care of the _____.

10. Because the staff worked hard, the evening _____ smoothly.

TALK *about the* topic

A. **Listen to the students talk about restaurants. Read each opinion. Then check (✓) who agrees with it.**

	Hannah	River	Mia	Manny
1. The quality of the food is more important than the ambience.	☐	☐	☐	☐
2. Ambience can really affect your feelings about the food.	☐	☐	☐	☐
3. A good waitstaff and nice lighting can influence your dining experience.	☐	☐	☐	☐

B. **Listen to the discussion again. Listen closely for the comments below. Check (✓) the discussion strategy the student uses.**

	Agreeing	Asking for clarification or confirmation	Paraphrasing
1. **Hannah:** "Can anyone explain it to me?"	☐	☐	☐
2. **River:** "He was trying to explain the difference between the relaxed experience of the guests, and the hard work of the staff."	☐	☐	☐
3. **Manny:** "I think he means that if you run a restaurant … "	☐	☐	☐
4. **River:** "You mean to say, if I have a burned steak I'm going to think it tastes great … "	☐	☐	☐
5. **Mia:** "OK. I can see that … "	☐	☐	☐

Discussion Strategy: Observe a group discussion and you're likely to hear **expressions of agreement** like *Uh-huh, Right, Yes, I agree, Exactly,* and *No doubt* to name a few. Agreeing is a great way to support another speaker, either in casual conversation or to build an alliance when an issue is being discussed.

C. **In small groups, discuss one or more of these topics. Try to use the discussion strategies you have learned.**

- Everyone wants "good food," but food preferences vary. How do you define good food? What would be your perfect meal in a restaurant?
- If you could open your own restaurant, what would it be like?

REVIEW *your* notes

Work with a partner. Use your notes to complete this outline of the lecture. Include information on topics and subtopics. Then work together to retell the main ideas.

I. Creating a positive dining experience — 2 major customer service concepts:

    1)

    2)

II. Creating ambience — factors to consider:

III. How to meet customer expectations:

IV. Brigade system:

    1) _____ = _____

    takes care of:

    2) _____ = _____

    takes care of:

V. Conclusions about Kate and Justin's experience:

    1)

    2)

TAKE THE UNIT TEST

Now you are ready to take the Unit Test.

# EXTEND *the* topic

Now you've learned a little about managing a restaurant. What about working directly with customers, or behind the scenes creating the menu? Listen and read to learn more about these and other aspects of the restaurant business.

 A. **Listen to a waiter with two decades of experience talk about what customers want. Discuss these questions with your classmates.**

1. Have you ever had a very bad restaurant experience? What happened?

2. Do you agree with the expression "the customer is always right"?

3. What should a restaurant do about a customer who has a problem with the food or service?

B. **Read about how marketing contributes to the success of a restaurant.**

A menu is a selling tool for a restaurant. It not only tells customers about the food and prices, but also reflects the restaurant's mission statement, or overall purpose. Look at these examples.

GREAT WALL EXPRESS WE PROVIDE "HARD TO RESIST," AFFORDABLE CHINESE MEALS FOR PEOPLE ON THE GO. LUNCH SPECIALS AND BOXED LUNCHES AVAILABLE DAILY 11:00 –2:00.

Fresh Feast Cafe
We serve home cooking at its finest. All of our food is made fresh daily using only the best local ingredients in season. Reasonably priced fare for those who care about what they eat.

Mario's Ristorante
Casual dining. We offer authentic, northern Italian food served in a family-friendly atmosphere. Suitable for all ages and all budgets.

A restaurant's mission statement should be reflected in its menu design. The type of paper, the artwork, the color, and the style can make a strong first impression on customers, influencing what they choose to order.

Work with a partner. Discuss what each restaurant is like. Then design a menu for one of the restaurants. What kind of menu design would best reflect the mission statement? Compare your designs with your classmates' designs.

" . . . And could I get three extra pickles on my sandwich?
And could you turn the music down? And the heat up?
And no ice in my soda. And . . . "

C. Research food professions.

The goal of a restaurant chef is to create delicious food. There are other creative positions in the restaurant industry as well. For example:

---> restaurant reviewer for a blog or a travel magazine

---> food photographer

---> graphic designer (for menus and advertisements)

---> interior designer (of the dining area)

Follow these steps.

1. Choose a food profession that interests you.

2. Research the responsibilities, training required, and average salary.

3. Prepare a short presentation for the class or a small group.

UNIT 5

How We Each Learn Best

CONNECT *to the* topic

We sometimes hear "Oh, she's really smart" or "He's so intelligent." But how often do we stop to consider what the term intelligent *actually means? Many people think a written intelligence test is the best way to find out how intelligent someone is. Many experts, however, have begun to understand that traditional written tests don't measure all types of intelligence. How would you describe an intelligent person?*

Read each statement. Decide if it describes you, then score it.
3 = This really describes me. 2 = This is me sometimes. 1 = This isn't me at all.

Statement   **Score:**

┄┄┄➤ I don't read instruction manuals—I like to figure out how things work.   _____

┄┄┄➤ I like working alone better than in a group.   _____

┄┄┄➤ I enjoy using my imagination.   _____

┄┄┄➤ I love to dance and listen to music.   _____

┄┄┄➤ I'm good at understanding other people's feelings.   _____

┄┄┄➤ I'd rather spend my time exploring nature than reading about it.   _____

┄┄┄➤ I know what I like and what I don't like.   _____

┄┄┄➤ I have a good sense of direction. I never get lost.   _____

┄┄┄➤ I like to use charts and graphs to get information quickly.   _____

Compare responses with a partner. What do they show about your personality or how you learn?

BUILD *your* vocabulary

A. The boldfaced words are from this unit's lecture on multiple intelligences. Listen to each sentence. Then guess the meaning of the boldfaced word. Work with a partner.

1. Some people don't think traditional IQ tests **accurately** determine intelligence. They believe other kinds of measurement are necessary.

2. To **assess** Darla's speaking ability, the teacher asked her to give an interpretation of a poem. After Darla finished, the teacher gave her a high score.

3. Ken is very **aware** of his own emotions and needs. He knows, for example, that being in a large room full of strangers makes him uncomfortable.

4. The new student has strong verbal intelligence. He **demonstrated** this by writing an excellent report and then presenting it to the class.

5. I have strong **kinesthetic** intelligence. I prefer "hands-on" learning—that is, learning by moving and doing.

6. Using **logic** is one sign of mathematical intelligence. While many people can work with numbers, not everyone can use reason.

7. My cousin can look at a map briefly and get a **mental** image of how the trails all connect.

8. Some educators reject the **notion** that standardized tests are unfair. They believe that this idea is simply wrong.

9. Ms. Kline gave the students two **options** to choose from: They could write a summary of the lecture, or they could make a chart of the key points.

10. Most schools **value** the ability to speak and write well more than they care about artistic or musical ability.

B. Now match each phrase with the correct meaning.

____ 1. **accurately** determine
____ 2. **assess** a student's ability
____ 3. be **aware** of
____ 4. **demonstrate** intelligence
____ 5. **kinesthetic** learning
____ 6. use **logic**
____ 7. **mental** image
____ 8. reject a **notion**
____ 9. give an **option**
____ 10. **value** the ability

a. *offer a choice in a situation*
b. *make a judgment; test*
c. *consider (the ability) important*
d. *learning by moving*
e. *correctly measure*
f. *a picture in the mind*
g. *not accept an idea*
h. *use sensible reasons*
i. *show ability or skill*
j. *realize something exists or is true*

C. *INTERACT WITH VOCABULARY!* **Work with a partner. Take turns saying the sentences. Notice the boldfaced words. Choose the best word to complete each sentence.**

1. First we'll be (go / going) **over** the theory of multiple intelligences.

2. The theory has had a major **impact** (on / for) teachers.

3. Keep (at / in) **mind** that some psychologists don't agree with the theory.

4. IQ (stands / stood) **for** "intelligence quotient."

5. No one in my family is **good** (at / on) taking tests.

6. We can **think** (of / for) *inter*personal as meaning between people and *intra*personal as meaning within one person.

7. A high IQ test score is typically **interpreted to** (mean / be) that the person is intelligent.

8. Doing a (various / variety) **of** activities instead of just one kind is a good teaching practice.

9. Some people are (sense / sensitive) **to** the colors around them.

10. This (brings / bring) **up** other issues, such as standardized tests.

FOCUS *your* attention

NUMBERED LISTS

A speaker often tells you how many ideas will be covered in a lecture. For example:

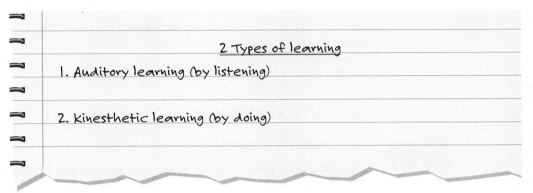

> There are **five steps** in the process . . .
> I'm going to present **two techniques** . . .
> I'm going to cover **three types** of learning styles . . .

One way to organize your notes is to write down the numbers and key phrases indicated by the speaker. Leave space in between to add short descriptions and details as you listen to the lecture.

Say you hear, *I'm going to present two types of learning: auditory learning—learning by listening—and kinesthetic learning—learning by doing.* Your notes might look like this:

<u>2 Types of learning</u>

1. Auditory learning (by listening)

2. Kinesthetic learning (by doing)

TRY IT OUT!

A. Listen to this excerpt from a lecture on teaching techniques. What numbers and phrases do you hear? Take notes below.

B. How did you organize your notes? Compare notes with a partner.

LISTEN *to the* lecture

BEFORE YOU LISTEN

You are about to listen to this unit's lecture on multiple intelligences. What do you think the term *multiple intelligences* means?

_____

LISTEN FOR MAIN IDEAS

A. **Close your book. Listen to the lecture and take notes.**

B. **Use your notes. Decide if the statements are *T* (true) or *F* (false), according to the lecture. Correct the false statements.**

____ 1. Psychologists know IQ tests are the best way to accurately measure intelligence.

____ 2. Dr. Gardner and others think of "an intelligence" as a strength a person has.

____ 3. People are all different. We all have different intelligences.

____ 4. A good teacher emphasizes verbal and mathematical intelligences because they are the most important.

____ 5. Teachers who accept the theory of multiple intelligences use a variety of teaching techniques.

____ 6. A written test is the best way for students to show that they understand a lesson.

LISTEN FOR DETAILS

A. **Close your book. Listen to the lecture again. Add details to your notes and correct any mistakes.**

B. **Use your notes. Choose the word or phrase that best completes each idea, based on the lecture.**

1. Having "intelligence" means _____.

   having a good education   being smart   having a strong ability in an area

2. A score of _____ on an intelligence test is average.

   130   100   113

3. One factor that can affect someone's IQ test score is _____.

   musical ability   cultural background   height

4. Someone who uses logic to solve problems has strong _____ intelligence.

   artistic   verbal   mathematical

5. When Ken watches movies, he pays more attention to the soundtrack than to what the actors say. He seems to have stronger _____ intelligence than _____ intelligence.

   musical / verbal   verbal / musical   kinesthetic / verbal

6. Someone with strong spatial intelligence would be good at _____.

   learning a new language   reading a map   doing something hands-on

7. Daniel is a good group leader. He works well with his classmates. He has strong _____ intelligence.

   kinesthetic   interpersonal   intrapersonal

8. Intrapersonal intelligence is directed toward _____.

   the group   the classroom   oneself

9. When Mrs. Sanchez has her students go outside and walk around, she is having them use _____ intelligence.

   artistic   kinesthetic   spatial

10. To assess her students, Mrs. Sanchez lets them choose any option they want as long as it is _____.

    written clearly   drawn well   about what she taught

TALK *about the* topic

A. Listen to the students talk about intelligence. Read each opinion. Then check (☑) who agrees with it.

	Qiang	Yhinny	Michael	May
1. A sculptor has talent, not intelligence.	☐	☐	☐	☐
2. Having a high IQ doesn't mean you're good at doing something.	☐	☐	☐	☐
3. The multiple intelligences theory is more useful than an IQ test.	☐	☐	☐	☐

B. Listen to the discussion again. Listen closely for the comments below. Check (☑) the discussion strategy the student uses.

	Expressing an opinion	Offering a fact or example	Asking for clarification or confirmation
1. **May:** "What do you mean?"	☐	☐	☐
2. **Yhinny:** "Can you give me an example?"	☐	☐	☐
3. **Michael:** "OK. So, for example, this guy Anthony in my history class … "	☐	☐	☐
4. **Qiang:** "But, he's intelligent in some other way, you think?"	☐	☐	☐
5. **May:** "I don't think education is for developing those talents. … I'm sorry, that's just how I see it."	☐	☐	☐

Discussion Strategy: In an academic setting, you have numerous opportunities to **express your opinions**—your thoughts, feelings, and positions. But while many opinions start with expressions like *I think, I believe* and *In my opinion*, only the interesting ones continue with facts, experiences, and other forms of support!

C. In small groups, discuss one or more of these topics. Try to use the discussion strategies you have learned.

- Think about how you learn. Which intelligences are strong for you?
- Teachers can guide students to use their more developed intelligences to help them learn more easily. When you were younger, was there something that was difficult for you to learn? What would have made it easier for you?
- Suppose you want to learn how to use a new camera. What would you do? Compare your approaches.

REVIEW *your* notes

Read your notes. How did you write down the important information? Work with a partner. Take turns explaining the ideas from the lecture as you complete these notes.

Def. of multiple intelligences:

Traditional way to measure intelligence:

Reasons some people don't like:

9 intelligences:

1)   6)
2)   7)
3)   8)
4)   9)
5)

2 effects of multiple intelligences theory in classroom:

1)

2)

Issue with standardized tests:

Now you are ready to take the Unit Test.

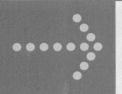

EXTEND *the* topic

Now that you've heard about other ways of defining intelligence, do you recognize other intelligences in yourself? Listen and read on to learn more about appreciating different strengths.

A. Listen as a guest speaker is introduced at a conference on being successful. Discuss these questions with a partner.

1. Do you know anyone like Zack who didn't do well in school, but was successful in another way?

2. What types of classroom activities might help a student like Zack? Think about his specific strengths.

B. Read about emotional intelligence.

"Do you think Janice is taking your suggestion to take the ball and run with it a little too far?"

Interpersonal intelligence is part of what is known as emotional intelligence. Someone with strong emotional intelligence often has strong leadership skills and can work well with others. He or she has a good sense of what other people are thinking and feeling, and can create harmony in a group. Emotional intelligence is beneficial in many contexts: at work, at school, and on sports teams. In fact, sports has inspired many expressions used to talk about leadership—and failure.

For example:

- "take the ball and run with it" means to take charge and go as far as you can
- "cover all the bases" means to be thorough
- "roll with the punches" means to adapt easily to new situations and challenges
- "strike out" means to fail
- "fumble" means to make a mistake
- "throw in the towel" means to quit

Discuss these questions with a partner.

----> Which of these sports phrases could be used to talk about someone you know who has strong emotional intelligence? What other words or phrases could be used to describe the person? Compare ideas.

----> Strong emotional intelligence is increasingly valued by companies. Do you think emotional intelligence should be a factor in getting hired? How might a company "test" for it?

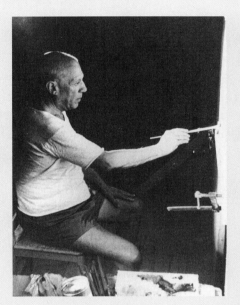 

What was an intelligence, or strength, of artist Pablo Picasso?
What about basketball star Michael Jordan?

C. Research cultural differences.

According to Harvard University's Dr. Howard Gardner, different cultures value different intelligences, and we are motivated to develop the intelligences that are important in our own culture. They will help us to be successful.

Follow these steps.

1. Write down the types of intelligences you think are most valued in your culture. Think about both the educational system and the skills that are important in daily life.

2. Choose another culture. Try to choose one that seems very different from yours. Talk to someone from that culture or use the Internet to find out what types of intelligences are valued.

3. Form groups and compare ideas.

UNIT 6

The Silk Road

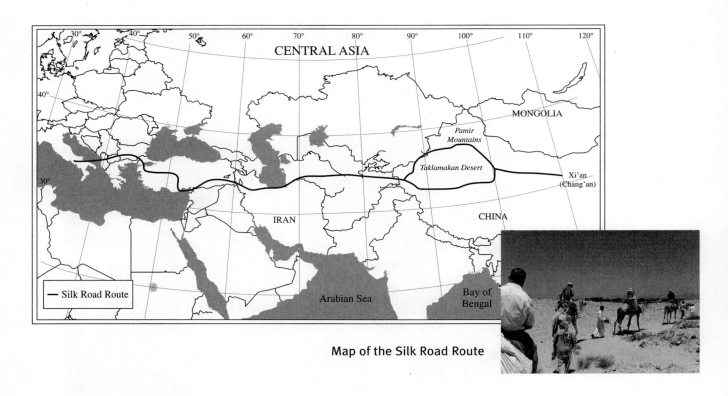

Map of the Silk Road Route

CONNECT *to the* topic

The Silk Road was a major trade route between China and Europe through Central Asia. Many of us have heard about Marco Polo using the Silk Road on his journey to China. But how many of us have thought about how difficult it was to travel this desolate terrain through Central Asia? Traders used caravans of camels through vast deserts and steep mountain ranges. They were always searching for the fastest and safest routes.

Work with a partner. Look at the map of the Silk Road. Follow the routes from Xi'an (formerly known as Chang'an) to Rome and Istanbul. Fill in the following names:

·····⟩ regions: Europe, Asia

·····⟩ countries: India, Italy, Turkey

·····⟩ cities: Dunhuang, Kashgar

·····⟩ desert: the Gobi Desert

Discuss which routes look easiest. Why?

BUILD *your* vocabulary

A. The boldfaced words are from this unit's lecture on the Silk Road. Listen to each sentence. Then guess the meaning of the boldfaced word.

1. The Silk Road was a large **network** of interconnected routes. People could travel between China and Rome through various roads that came together.

2. Some traders stayed on the northern route of the Silk Road. Others took an **alternate** route to the south. Both routes led to the Mediterranean Sea.

3. The Han **Dynasty** controlled China for nearly 400 years. Under this powerful family's control, China developed trade with Europe.

4. During the Han Dynasty, the Chinese army was engaged in a **conflict** with Mongol invaders from the north. They fought for many years.

5. The army needed to **recruit** more fighters so that it would have enough soldiers to defend northern China.

6. In 138 BCE, Emperor Wudi sent a group to western China, where the group's leader was held prisoner for a **decade**. The emperor was surprised when the leader returned after those ten years.

7. As the Silk Road developed, the Romans and the Chinese were pushing east and west, **respectively**. In other words, the Romans went east toward China, while the Chinese went west toward Rome.

8. The years of the Tang Dynasty were the **peak** period for the Silk Road. It was most heavily used during that time.

9. The Chinese city of Chang'an (now called Xi'an) was very **prosperous**. Lots of money and goods flowed into Chang'an from many countries.

10. Around 900 CE, trade along the Silk Road started to **decline** sharply. Trade decreased because ongoing fighting made it unsafe to travel.

B. Now complete each sentence with the correct word.

decade	decline	network	prosperous	recruit

1. The government needed to _____ more men for the army.

2. Traders traveled various directions through a _____ of routes.

3. Many people became _____ and could buy luxury goods.

4. Trade increased for hundreds of years, but then started to _____.

5. Instead of saying "the years 1990 to 1999," people often refer to that _____ as "the 90s."

alternate	conflict	dynasties	peak	respectively

6. A _____ between two countries can last for many years.

7. China was ruled by different _____ for thousands of years.

8. There were many traders in Rome and Chang'an—in other words, from Italy and China, _____.

9. During _____ travel on the Silk Road, large caravans of camels with traders left Chang'an daily.

10. A bad sandstorm developed in the desert, and so the traders took a(n) _____ route.

C. *INTERACT WITH VOCABULARY!* **Read the sentences with a partner. Notice the boldfaced words. Then choose a pair of particles from the box to complete the each sentence.**

from / in	to / in	in / for	of / of

1. The Han Dynasty was _____ **power** _____ several hundred **years**.

2. The routes **led** _____ trade centers _____ **Europe**.

3. There are different **estimates** _____ the total **length** _____ the Silk Road.

4. Romans wanted luxury goods _____ **China**, silk _____ **particular**.

through / in	both / and	against / from

5. It was difficult to **defend** China _____ the Mongol invaders _____ **the north**.

6. The traders **passed** _____ many small towns _____ **Central Asia**.

7. The traders exchanged _____ goods _____ trade secrets.

FOCUS *your* attention

DATES AND NUMBERS

Many history lectures include dates, numbers, and chronologies—or series of events. In a lecture like this, it is important to keep track of the key idea or information associated with each date or number you hear.

CE stands for "Common Era." It is a relatively new term that is being used more and more, and it is expected to eventually replace *AD*. *AD* is an abbreviation for the Latin phrase "Anno Domini," which means "the year of the Lord" in English. CE and AD have the same meaning. 2008 CE = 2008 AD. *BCE* stands for "Before the Common Era." It is expected to eventually replace *BC*, which means "Before Christ." *BC* and *BCE* also have the same meaning.

Here are examples of how these terms might sound:

> 206 BCE = Two-oh-six b-c-e
> 1368 CE = thirteen-sixty-eight c-e

One way to organize your notes is to write dates, key phrases, and details in separate columns. Leave space to add to your notes as you listen to the lecture.

For example:

China

Dates	Key phrase	Details
206 BCE– 220 CE	Han Dynasty	Silk Road developed
618–907 CE	Tang Dynasty	peak period of the Silk Road
1368 CE	Ming Dynasty	in power; trade drops off

TRY IT OUT!

A. Listen to this excerpt from a history lecture. What dates and events do you hear? What details? Take notes.

B. Compare notes with a partner. Answer the questions.

LISTEN *to the* lecture

BEFORE YOU LISTEN

You are about to listen to this unit's lecture on the Silk Road. During the time of the Silk Road, no one called it "the Silk Road." The name was given by German geographer Ferdinand von Richthofen in the nineteenth century. Why do you think he chose the name "the Silk Road"?

_____

LISTEN FOR MAIN IDEAS

A. **Close your book. Listen to the lecture and take notes.**

B. **Use your notes. Answer the questions, based on the lecture. Circle *a*, *b*, or *c*.**

1. What is the main topic of the lecture?

    a. why Chinese goods were popular

    b. how the Silk Road developed

    c. where the Silk Road was located

2. What was the main reason the Han government wanted to head west initially?

    a. to sell gold

    b. to get horses

    c. to sell spices

3. Who conducted most of the trade?

    a. traders from China

    b. traders from Rome

    c. traders from Central Asia

4. What two things did traders try to avoid?

    a. bad people, bad weather

    b. bad weather, bad roads

    c. bad roads, low-quality goods

5. What were the two main reasons trade on the Silk Road stopped?

    a. Silk was no longer popular, and luxury goods were too expensive.

    b. The weather was too dangerous, and there were too many robberies.

    c. There was too much fighting, and traders started to prefer ships.

Turkey, once at the west end of the Silk Road, is still a major crossroads for trade and culture today.

LISTEN FOR DETAILS

A. Close your book. Listen to the lecture again. Add details to your notes and correct any mistakes.

B. Use your notes. Decide if the statements below are *T* (true) or *F* (false), according to the lecture. Correct the false statements.

_____ 1. The Silk Road was a major trade route for about 1,000 years.

_____ 2. Trade between Europe and China increased significantly in 200 BCE.

_____ 3. Both Rome and Istanbul are mentioned as important trade centers.

_____ 4. The speaker gave an estimated distance of 5,000 miles (8,000 kilometers) for the Silk Road.

_____ 5. In 138 BCE, Emperor Wudi of the Han Dynasty sent a group to western China to expand trade.

_____ 6. Traders wanted to avoid the Taklamakan Desert.

_____ 7. Most of the traders went short distances.

_____ 8. At the Silk Road's peak popularity, about 2 million people lived in Chang'an, including 6,000 foreigners.

_____ 9. By the 600s, the Tang Dynasty had lost control.

_____ 10. Trade on the Silk Road stopped by 1368.

TALK *about the* topic

A. Listen to the students talk about the Silk Road. Read each comment. Then check (✔) the student who makes the comment.

	Ayman	Molly	Rob	Alana
1. "I'd heard of the Silk Road before, but I had no idea it was so complicated!"	☐	☐	☐	☐
2. "I think I got the general idea—that China wanted goods from Europe, and Europe wanted goods from China . . ."	☐	☐	☐	☐
3. "It was probably a pretty dangerous job, too, I mean, if you think about it . . ."	☐	☐	☐	☐

B. Listen to the discussion again. Listen closely for the comments below. Check (✔) the discussion strategy the student uses.

	Asking for opinions or ideas	Offering a fact or example	Asking for clarification or confirmation
1. **Alana:** "So, do you guys think the Silk Road is famous because of the goods traded . . . ?"	☐	☐	☐
2. **Rob:** "Essentially, it was about trade, right?"	☐	☐	☐
3. **Ayman:** "Oh yeah, like Central Asian traders. They had a very important job."	☐	☐	☐
4. **Alana:** "Kind of like businesspeople today . . ."	☐	☐	☐

C. In small groups, discuss one or more of these topics. Try to use the discussion strategies you have learned.

- Silk Road traders took many risks. Compare those to risks in travel and business today.
- What does Molly mean by "I guess not that much has changed in the past 2,000 years!"? Do you agree with her?
- During the peak period, Chang'an was an important trade center, and people from many different cultures came into contact. What cities are like this now? Compare them.

REVIEW *your* notes

Work with a partner. Ask each other questions about the years presented in the lecture. What years and numbers did you write down in your notes? Do you know why they are important? Then consider the reasons why events occurred. For example, why did Rome want to develop routes to China? Try using some of these phrases in your questions:

> What happened in . . . ?　　　What is . . . ?
>
> When was the (Tang) Dynasty?　What caused . . . ?
>
> How many . . . ?　　　　　　　Why did . . . ?
>
> When did . . . ?

Add information to this timeline to help you summarize the main ideas of the lecture.

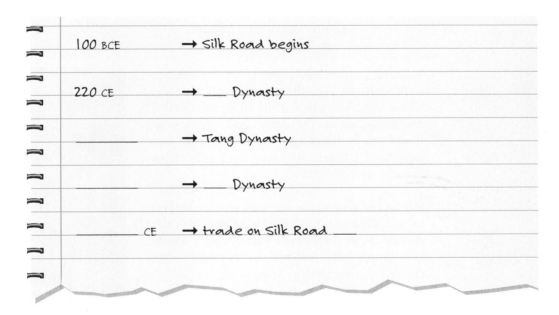

Now you are ready to take the Unit Test.

> **Tip!**
>
> Remember: A timeline is like a "snapshot" of how historic dates and events fit together. It tells the whole story in just a glance!

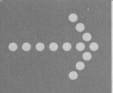

EXTEND *the* topic

Learning about historical events and places like the Silk Road can be inspiring. Listen and read more about how the Silk Road lives on today.

A. **Listen to a travel TV guide talk as she plans her next stop along the Silk Road. Then discuss these questions with your classmates.**

1. What "exotic" foods have you tried? Is there anything you wouldn't eat?

2. What does "adventure traveler" mean? What kind of traveler are you?

3. What do you think about traveling with the help of a guide?

B. **You have learned about the economic impact of the Silk Road. Now read about the cultural impact.**

Some of the greatest "imports" of the Silk Road were cultural. Buddhism was introduced to China from India by traders along the northern route. By about the early first century BCE, Buddhism had had a major influence on many aspects of Chinese life, including architecture, the arts, and education.

Literature also made its way along the trade routes. One example is the Effendi folktales, stories about the Effendi Nasreddin, a Muslim folk hero. The Effendi, a common man, cleverly points out the weaknesses of those in power. In one story, he needs to add a second floor to his house. He borrows money from a rich man, who then demands that the Effendi give him the second floor. In response, the Effendi starts to tear down the first floor. The rich man begs the Effendi to let him buy the first floor, which the Effendi only agrees to for a lot of money! These tales traveled from the Middle East to Central Asia to China, and they still survive today.

A shrine near the Mogao caves in China

Work with a partner. Discuss the following questions.

1. Do you know any folktales similar to this one about the Effendi Nasreddin?

2. Like the Silk Road, globalization has had an impact on many countries—for example, in the development of world music. What type of music do you and your friends like? What are the origins of that music?

3. What other "foreign" influences are there in your life? Consider things such as foods, fashions, movies, and hairstyles.

C. **Research a topic from along the Silk Road. Choose from the following list. Prepare a short presentation for the class or a small group.**

    ·····> a famous person associated with the Silk Road, such as Marco Polo, Sir Aurel Stein, Kublai Khan, or Ferdinand von Richthofen

    ·····> Chinese art and architecture from the Han or Tang Dynasty

    ·····> the empire of Parthia in Persia, or the Roman Empire

    ·····> how silk is made

UNIT 7

Team Building

CONNECT *to the* topic

We live in an era of globalization. With globalization comes more multiculturalism and diversity in the workplace. It's common now for companies to recruit employees from various backgrounds. These employees may have very different worldviews, social rules, and styles of communicating. A good manager needs to know how to use these differences to the advantage of the team.

Consider your own values. Read the statements. Check (☑) those you agree with.

┈┈➤ I pay attention to time. I like to do one task, then another, and finish on schedule. _____

┈┈➤ I care more about family and friends than about my job or career. _____

┈┈➤ When someone is talking, I don't like to interrupt. _____

┈┈➤ Personal freedom is very important to me. _____

┈┈➤ A manager should always be "in charge," even in social situations outside of work. _____

┈┈➤ Sometimes, it's OK to speak up and disagree with your manager. _____

┈┈➤ It's easier to work by myself than with a group. _____

┈┈➤ My education is more valuable than my actual skills or work habits. _____

Compare responses with a partner.

BUILD *your* vocabulary

A. The boldfaced words below are from this unit's lecture on team building. Listen to each sentence. Do you know any synonyms for the boldfaced words?

1. The team needed to **accomplish** a certain amount each week in order to finish the contract on time.

2. One **challenge** a manager faces is how to build a strong team. This is often a difficult part of the manager's job.

3. An **effective** manager knows how to approach employees so that they feel motivated to do their best work.

4. After the manager hired new employees, she planned several social activities to **enhance** the team feeling.

5. A good **practice** is to always be polite to your coworkers.

6. The first **project** was easy, but the one the manager just assigned is harder.

7. The manager of the advertising company had to **pull together** a design team quickly. Fortunately, she had good organizational skills.

8. Managers should **resolve** small conflicts before they become big problems.

9. E-mail was **sufficient** for most office communication. But when it wasn't enough, a meeting was held.

10. At the end of the meeting, the manager gave a **summary** of his main points.

11. Good communication within a team is **vital** to its success. Without it, the team will fail.

12. Because the topic of business is so broad, it's helpful to **zero in on** one aspect: management.

B. Now match the boldfaced word with its definition.

1.	**challenge**	a.	to organize
2.	**practice**	b.	a habit, a way of doing something
3.	**project**	c.	to pay special attention to
4.	**pull together**	d.	a large planned piece of work
5.	**zero in on**	e.	something difficult that requires effort to do
6.	**accomplish**	f.	to succeed in doing something after trying hard

7.	**effective**	g.	producing a desired result
8.	**enhance**	h.	as much as needed
9.	**resolve**	i.	to improve or to make something better
10.	**sufficient**	j.	a short statement of key information
11.	**summary**	k.	extremely important or necessary
12.	**vital**	l.	to fix a problem

C. *INTERACT WITH VOCABULARY!* Work with a partner. Read the sentences in Column A and discuss the meanings of the boldfaced phrases. Then read sentences 1–5 aloud as your partner fills in the blanks in Column B. Switch roles for 6–10.

Column A	Column B
1. The **chemistry between** the two designers was bad. They didn't work well together.	1. The **chemistry** _____ the two designers was bad. They didn't work well together.
2. The team's common goal is to complete the contract **on time**.	2. The team's common goal is to complete the contract _____ time.
3. Team members are **responsible for** a task, so it's their job to do it.	3. Team members are **responsible** _____ a task, so it's their job to do it.
4. Last week, we got **started on** styles of management. Today, we'll finish up.	4. Last week, we got **started** _____ styles of management. Today, we'll finish up.
5. A manager decides which employee is best **suited for** each task.	5. A manager decides which employee is best **suited** _____ each task.
6. Dan's easygoing personality allows him to **fit in** well with everyone.	6. Dan's easygoing personality allows him to **fit** _____ well with everyone.
7. **In summary**, good communication helps build a team.	7. _____ **summary**, good communication helps build a team.
8. Some employees consider meetings an **interference with** their other work.	8. Some employees consider meetings an **interference** _____ their other work.
9. Unclear e-mails can **lead to** big misunderstandings.	9. Unclear e-mails can **lead** _____ big misunderstandings.
10. Face-to-face meetings can be **a waste of time**. A call can be quicker.	10. Face-to-face meetings can be **a waste** _____ **time**. A call can be quicker.

FOCUS *your* attention

SYMBOLS AND ABBREVIATIONS

As you listen to a lecture, it's important to be able to take notes quickly. One helpful technique is to use symbols and abbreviations. You can create your own, or you can use standard ones. For example:

Symbol or abbreviation	Meaning
e.g. or ex.	for example
etc.	additional persons or things
i.e.	in other words
&	and
@	at
↑	increase
↓	decrease
#	amount OR number of
=	is OR equals
≠	isn't OR doesn't equal
x	number of times (*2x*)
→	causes OR results in
?	question

Say you hear *The manager needed to make some changes—for example, an increase in the number of people on the team.* Your notes might look like this:

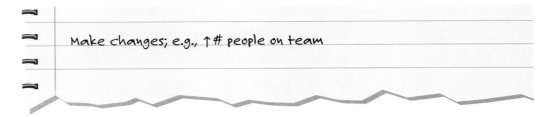

Make changes; e.g., ↑# people on team

TRY IT OUT!

A. Listen to this excerpt from a seminar about teamwork in business. Take notes using symbols and abbreviations.

B. Compare notes with a partner. What symbols and abbreviations did you use?

LISTEN *to the* lecture

BEFORE YOU LISTEN

You are about to listen to this unit's lecture on building a team in business. What qualities should a good manager possess?

_____

LISTEN FOR MAIN IDEAS

A. Close your book. Listen to the lecture and take notes.

B. Use your notes. Answer the questions, based on the lecture. Circle *a*, *b*, or *c*.

1. Which best describes how a team is different from a group?

    a. A team's members may be strangers.

    b. A team's members may know each other.

    c. A team's members share a common goal.

2. What does the manager at RZDesign need to focus on?

    a. hiring new employees

    b. building a strong team very quickly

    c. winning a big contract

3. What aspect of team building does the speaker mainly discuss?

    a. holding face-to-face meetings

    b. planning social activities for the team

    c. building trust within the team

4. What does "team chemistry" mean?

    a. how hard the people on a team work

    b. how the personalities of the people fit together

    c. how team members decide to communicate

5. Which of the following statements would the speaker agree with?

    a. A good manager should always plan plenty of social activities.

    b. A good manager should plan social activities based on personalities.

    c. A good manager should only plan two social activities.

LISTEN FOR DETAILS

A. Close your book. Listen to the lecture again. Add details to your notes and correct any mistakes.

B. Use your notes. Decide if the statements below are *T* (true) or *F* (false), according to the lecture. Correct the false statements.

____ 1. The speaker thinks there are similarities between a good coach and a good manager.

____ 2. All of the members of Tina's team were just hired.

____ 3. The team's common goal is to complete their contract within ten months.

____ 4. Tina's first step is to assess the skills of the employees.

____ 5. Tina assigns roles after she decides who is best suited for each task.

____ 6. Tina tells her team that e-mail is the best way to resolve any conflicts.

____ 7. The speaker seems to agree with Tina that face-to-face meetings are important.

____ 8. Tina keeps team meetings short because she is busy.

____ 9. The speaker mentions Brazil as a country where it's important to build relationships first.

____ 10. The speaker concludes that a manager needs to plan a lot of social activities.

TALK *about the* topic

A. Listen to the students talk about the team building lecture. Read each opinion. Then check (☑) who disagrees with it.

	River	Mia	Manny	Hannah
1. The idea of team chemistry is uninteresting.	☐	☐	☐	☐
2. This study group has poor chemistry.	☐	☐	☐	☐
3. Face-to-face meetings are easy to make time for.	☐	☐	☐	☐
4. Team-building activities are enjoyable.	☐	☐	☐	☐

B. Listen to the discussion again. Listen closely for the comments below. Check (☑) the discussion strategy the student uses.

	Disagreeing	Keeping the discussion on topic	Trying to reach a consensus
1. **Mia:** "I suggest we just go around and cover the seven steps to team building, OK?"	☐	☐	☐
2. **Mia:** "Anyway, back to the steps."	☐	☐	☐
3. **Hannah:** "Really? That seems like the fun part to me."	☐	☐	☐
4. **Manny:** "What do you say we take a break and refill—to build our team?"	☐	☐	☐

> **Discussion Strategy:** Getting a group to **reach a consensus**, or agree, can be challenging. One approach is to use questions to identify areas of agreement ("So, when is everyone free to meet again?"). You can follow up by making suggestions based on feedback ("Sounds like Sunday is open for everyone—does that work?").

C. In small groups, discuss one or more of these topics. Try to use the discussion strategies you have learned.

- Based on your own experiences, what helps create good chemistry?
- In your opinion, how important are social activities?
- Think of someone you trust. Why do you trust this person? Be specific.

REVIEW *your* notes

Paraphrase means to say something in your own words. You can also paraphrase what someone else has said to make sure you have understood the information correctly. Work with a partner. Use your notes to paraphrase the main ideas of the lecture. Here are some expressions you can use:

> *I'm not sure I understand. Are you saying . . . ?*
> *It sounds like you are saying . . . Does that mean . . . ?*
> *You mentioned . . . Does that mean . . . ?*
> *Can you give me some examples of what you mean by . . . ?*

Compare the symbols and abbreviations in your notes. Then compare your notes with those below.

Team Building—good mgmt practice

team ≠ group

1. common goal

2. depend on ea. other

3. responsible for accomplishments

    ex. sports team + coach = strong team

    ex. RZDesign—ad co.—ad campaign (6 mos) = goal

Steps

    1. go over all work

    2. assess skills

    3. hold team mtgs: discuss project & assign roles

    4. ID challenge: bldg trust

    5. build trust → comm. + chemistry

    6. meet face-to-face (short)—discuss + resolve problems

    7. plan activities → relax together

        ex. S. America & Asia: build relations 1st v. U.S.: work 1st

        dep. on cultural backgrounds

Now you are ready to take the Unit Test.

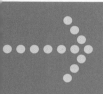

EXTEND *the* topic

So, as you've seen, building trust can be complicated. For new hires and experienced managers alike, developing productive professional relationships takes skill, as the following activities show.

 A. Listen to this call to a career help hotline. Discuss these questions with your classmates.

1. Imagine that you are a new hire at a big company. Someone who has been at the company a long time is causing problems for you. What do you do?

2. What do you think is the best way to resolve conflicts at work? At school? At home?

B. Read about how cultures perceive time differently.

Deborah Mackin, in her book *The Team Building Tool Kit*, points out that team meetings can be more effective if team members come to meetings on time. However, cultures vary in attitudes toward time. A good manager needs to consider the cultural backgrounds of team members. People from some cultures, such as the United States, the United Kingdom, and Japan, prefer to begin a meeting promptly at the scheduled time. Lateness is considered disrespectful. In contrast, in other cultures, such as France and Mexico, the schedule isn't as important as the interaction between people. Meetings start and end at flexible times, as needed. Lateness isn't considered impolite.

People's attitudes about time are often reflected in their language. In English there are many expressions related to time such as: *spend time, kill time, take time, give me a little of your time, budget one's time, invest time in, and time is money.* In many English-speaking cultures, time *is* like money. If you're late, you're "costing" everyone else.

Work in groups. Discuss the following questions.

⟶ Do you think of time as something to spend, waste, or run out of?

⟶ What does it mean to be "on time" or "late" in your culture? Think about various situations, such as school, work, parties, family gatherings, and meeting friends.

C. **Research a company's culture. Every company has its own culture. It conducts business based on its philosophy and core values—what it believes in.**

Follow these steps.

1. Choose a company you're interested in. Some ideas:
   Starbucks
   Avon
   Google
   Sony
   Any other high-profile company

2. Go to the company's website. Read its mission statement. Search different links to find out what the company is like. Decide if it's a company you would like to work for.

3. Prepare a presentation about the company and why you would or wouldn't like to work there.

4. In small groups, compare the cultures of the companies you researched.

ARCHITECTURE
Frank Gehry

Clockwise from left: Frank Gehry's Dancing House, Prague; Daigoji in Japan; Maracanã in Brazil

CONNECT *to the* topic

Picture a building you have stopped to admire. What attracted you to it? The shape? The windows? The colors? Something about its architecture, no doubt. Architecture—or design—draws on many fields: art, engineering, mathematics, even philosophy and politics. Each comes into play as an architect designs a building. Long ago, the Roman architect Vitruvius said a building must be strong, functional, and beautiful. These three principles of good architecture still guide us today.

Work with a partner. For each building pictured above, answer these questions.

> What aspects of the building's design do you like or dislike?

> What do you think the building is used for?

> What features make it seem strong enough to last a long time?

> What are some of your favorite buildings? Why?

BUILD *your* vocabulary

A. The boldfaced words are from this unit's lecture on architect Frank Gehry. Listen to each sentence. Then choose the phrase that goes with the boldfaced word.

____ 1. Architects consider the **aesthetics** of the buildings they design. They want people to find the buildings not only beautiful to look at but also enjoyable to be inside.

____ 2. The **foundation** of architecture today is based on the fundamentals of the past.

____ 3. The architect Frank Gehry is **inspirational**. He pushes other architects to explore new ideas.

____ 4. The **intended use** or purpose of a mall is a place to shop. For example, a café's intended use is as a place to eat.

____ 5. To say a building is structurally **sound** means that it is built to last a long time.

     a. *causing others to do or produce something*
     b. *the basis; the ideas that support something*
     c. *reason for the building*
     d. *artistic value*
     e. *in good condition; strong*

____ 6. Frank Gehry is noteworthy because of his **dynamic** style. His designs are very creative and unusual.

____ 7. A building must serve the needs and purposes of the people who use it. If the building does this, then the architect has **met the objective**.

____ 8. Aesthetics is a difficult **principle** to agree on because people have their own taste.

____ 9. Frank Gehry's designs often use irregular angles. It's important to **stress**, however, that the designs are still structurally sound.

____ 10. Frank Gehry was resourceful because he liked to **utilize** chain-link fence, plywood, sheet metal, and other building materials that were easily available to him.

     f. *achieved the goal*
     g. *rule or set of ideas*
     h. *to use something effectively*
     i. *exciting; interesting; full of energy*
     j. *to emphasize*

B. *INTERACT WITH VOCABULARY!* **Work with a partner. Notice the boldfaced words. Take turns completing each sentence with the correct form of the word. Read the completed sentences aloud. Review any words you don't understand.**

aesthetic	aesthetically	aesthetics

1. One of the basic **principles of** architecture is to consider the _____ of a building—for example the materials, lighting, and shape.

2. One _____ **consideration of** a structure's design is shape. The shape of the Arc de Triomphe in Paris, for example, is very strong and commanding. It is difficult to design a structure that is _____ **pleasing to** everyone.

distinct	distinguish

3. Frank Gehry has a _____ style, especially his **use of** irregular shapes

4. It's not difficult to _____ his work **from that of** other architects.

innovation	innovative	innovator

5. Frank Gehry is considered an _____. Trying new ideas was **at the foundation of** his designs.

6. An _____ architect doesn't follow traditional **styles of** building design.

7. A fairly recent _____ in architecture includes an **emphasis on** "going green," which means designing with the environment in mind.

sculptor	sculpture

8. The Fish Dance restaurant in Kobe, Japan, **looks like** a gigantic _____ of a fish.

9. I can't remember the name of the _____, but I liked how she **experimented with** shapes.

FOCUS *your* attention

EMPHASIS

During a lecture, you hear a lot of information quickly. Lecturers will often use signal phrases or emphasize words to focus your attention on important information. If they want to check in to see if you are following along, lecturers may cue you with questions. For example:

> Signaling emphasis
>
> To highlight what I've said so far . . .
>
> I want to emphasize that . . .
>
> I want to stress . . .
>
> It's important to understand . . .
>
> The fundamental point is . . .
>
> What I'm saying is . . .
>
> Checking in
>
> Is everyone clear on this?
>
> Is this clear?
>
> Are there any questions?
>
> Are you with me?

Say you hear *I want to stress that architecture is both an art and a science. . . . There are many factors to consider in the design of a building. . . . Are you with me?* Your notes might look like this:

— Architecture = an art and a science

— When designing a bldg: many factors to consider

TRY IT OUT!

A. **Listen to this excerpt from an architecture class. Which signal phrases and cues does the speaker use? Take notes. Underline the important information.**

B. **Compare notes with a partner.**

LISTEN *to the* lecture

BEFORE YOU LISTEN

You are about to listen to this unit's lecture on Frank Gehry. Check (☑) the top three considerations you think an architect should keep in mind when designing a building.

____ location   ____ colors   ____ use of recycled or environmentally responsible materials

____ size   ____ energy use

____ cost   ____ number of windows

LISTEN FOR MAIN IDEAS

A. **Close your book. Listen to the lecture and take notes.**

B. **Use your notes. Answer the questions, based on the lecture. Circle *a*, *b*, or *c*.**

1. How is architecture both a science and an art?

    a. Buildings must look nice from the outside and the inside.

    b. Buildings must be strong and beautiful.

    c. Buildings must protect people from bad weather.

2. Why does the speaker mention Vitruvius?

    a. to show that the principles of architecture change

    b. to show that Gehry's work is based on principles from long ago

    c. to show how styles in architecture change

3. What aspect of Gehry's work does the lecture mainly focus on?

    a. his building style in the 1970s

    b. examples of his work around the world

    c. his distinctive style

4. Why does Gehry use bright, bold colors?

    a. He wants to be playful.

    b. He's concerned about the environment.

    c. He wants his buildings to be strong.

5. Why did Gehry develop his dynamic style?

    a. He liked to experiment with building houses.

    b. Other architects didn't agree with his ideas.

    c. Traditional architecture didn't allow him to be creative enough.

6. What is the main reason the speaker likes Gehry?

    a. because Gehry understands traditional values in architecture

    b. because Gehry is innovative and resourceful

    c. because Gehry has designed many different buildings

LISTEN FOR DETAILS

A. **Close your book. Listen to the lecture again. Add details to your notes and correct any mistakes.**

B. **Use your notes. Decide if the statements below are *T* (true) or *F* (false), according to the lecture. Correct the false statements.**

____ 1. Designing buildings is both an art and a science.

____ 2. An example of a building being sound is one that protects people from bad weather.

____ 3. The speaker says that the intended use of a library is as a place to learn.

____ 4. Everyone agrees on aesthetics because styles in architecture don't change much.

____ 5. Plywood and sheet metal are examples of simple building materials Gehry used in the 1970s.

____ 6. The main reason Gehry used chain-link fence was that he thought it was beautiful.

____ 7. The speaker is worried that the Vitra Building in Germany might fall down because it doesn't look sound.

____ 8. Gehry used irregular shapes and angles to see what was possible from an engineering standpoint.

____ 9. The speaker believes Gehry thinks more like an engineer than an artist.

____ 10. Gehry thinks of buildings as sculptures that people interact with.

TALK about the topic

A. Listen to the students talk about Frank Gehry. Read each opinion. Then check (☑) who disagrees with it.

		Michael	Yhinny	May	Qiang
1.	Frank Gehry is one of the greatest architects ever.	☐	☐	☐	☐
2.	Frank Gehry will be forgotten by history.	☐	☐	☐	☐
3.	Frank Gehry's engineering abilities are put to good use.	☐	☐	☐	☐
4.	I'm a Frank Gehry enthusiast.	☐	☐	☐	☐

B. Listen to the discussion again. Listen closely for the comments below. Check (☑) the discussion strategy the student uses.

		Asking for opinions or ideas	Agreeing	Disagreeing
1.	**Yhinny:** "What? I wouldn't say that."	☐	☐	☐
2.	**Michael:** "I mean, I hate to disagree, but … "	☐	☐	☐
3.	**May:** "OK, then what would you say about his engineering abilities—can you say he's noteworthy for that?"	☐	☐	☐
4.	**Michael:** "OK, sure, I can see that."	☐	☐	☐
5.	**Michael:** "Why doesn't he put those abilities to use in a more practical way? Like building bridges?"	☐	☐	☐

C. In small groups, discuss one or more of these topics. Try to use the discussion strategies you have learned.

- Yhinny says that Frank Gehry's buildings are all over the world. What is her point?
- Michael suggests that someone like Frank Gehry should use his skills in practical ways like designing bridges rather than for designing aesthetically pleasing buildings. Do you agree?
- Some say Frank Gehry doesn't pay enough attention to the environment. Would these students agree with this criticism? Would you?

REVIEW *your* notes

Work with a partner. Use your notes. Work together to complete the outline below. Then retell the main ideas of the lecture in your own words.

I. 3 principles from Vitruvius: Ex.'s/Details:

   A.

   B.

   C.

II. 3 features of Gehry's style: Ex.'s/Details:

   A.

   B.

   C.

III. Ex.'s of his work:

IV. Reason(s) Gehry developed his style:

V. Reason(s) speaker likes Gehry:

TAKE THE UNIT TEST

Now you are ready to take the Unit Test.

Tip!

When a speaker "checks in," this is your chance to clarify anything you don't understand.

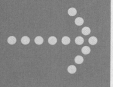

EXTEND *the* topic

Frank Gehry is just one of many who've left their mark on the world through architecture. Listen and read on to learn about impacts of architecture around the world.

 A. Listen to this excerpt from a TV show about unusual architecture around the world. Discuss these questions with your classmates.

1. Do you think "Reversible Destiny Architecture" is a good idea? What are the main advantages and disadvantages?

2. Would you like to try to spend a weekend in an apartment like this? Why or why not?

3. Do you have better ideas on how to live a long life?

B. Some people have criticized Frank Gehry for not being "green" enough in his designs—that is, for not paying enough attention to the environment. There are many ways to be "green." Read about a few in the article below.

Going green

Some companies "go green" by requiring employees to recycle plastics, glass, cans, and paper. They provide showers and bicycles so that employees can ride to work. They use solar-heated hot water in their buildings.

Shoppers and diners try to buy locally produced food when possible. They consider the distance the food had to travel to get to them.

And for those who want to keep up with the latest fashions, there's clothing made from eco-friendly materials such as soy, hemp, and bamboo, plus jackets, belts, and messenger bags made from recycled plastics. There's also fun jewelry made from seeds and shells. Lots of choices out there, and more coming every day!

There are also little things at home that add up: disconnect electronics—iPods, cell phones, laptops—from chargers as soon as they're "juiced"; use cloth bags for shopping; take shorter showers; and turn off the water while brushing your teeth.

Work with a partner to answer the following questions.

1. What are other ways to "go green"?

2. There are many jobs in the "green economy," including environmental engineer, environmental lawyer, "green" architect, solar installer, bicycle repair person, bicycle shop owner, and small restaurateur of locally grown food. Do "green jobs" appeal to you?

The Shoe, a shoe repair shop in Bakersfield, California

C. **Research one of the following topics on architecture.**

····> Styles in architecture: Choose a style, such as art deco or Bauhaus. Find out the key features of the style. Prepare a five-minute presentation.

····> Mimetic architecture: In mimetic architecture, a building is designed to advertise the business. For example, The Shoe in Bakersfield, California, looks like a big shoe and is a shoe repair shop. This style of architecture peaked in the 1930s, but interesting examples still exist today. Use the keywords *mimetic architecture* to find other fun examples to share with your classmates.

Building Immunity

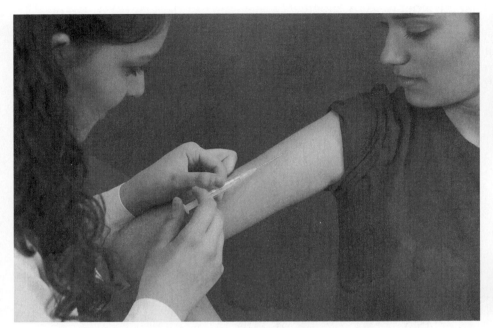

CONNECT *to the* **topic**

Do you consider yourself healthy? What does it take to be healthy? Good food? Laughter? Protection from disease? Public health officials are concerned with your health as well as that of the entire community. They look at ways to prevent diseases and promote health so that everyone can live healthier lives.

Here are some factors that affect your health. With a partner, add at least three more.

drink clean water	*get enough sleep*	_____
breathe clean air	*have access to medical care*	_____
eat healthy food	*live in good housing*	_____
get a lot of exercise		

Now answer these questions with your partner.

┄┄┄> What do you do to stay healthy?

┄┄┄> How many hours do you usually sleep at night?

┄┄┄> Do you travel? What special things do you do to stay healthy while traveling?

BUILD *your* vocabulary

A. The boldfaced words are from this unit's lecture on building immunity. Listen to each sentence. Then match the definition below to the boldfaced word.

_____ 1. When people move to a new place, some have trouble **adapting to** that new environment. They get sick because they're not accustomed to it.

_____ 2. A **contagious** disease—for example, the chicken pox—can spread quickly through a school. First one student gets it, then another, and so on.

_____ 3. My husband has a strong immune system, so he rarely gets sick. He's able to **resist** the germs and bacteria that could harm him.

a. adjusting to	b. fight off	c. passed by touch or through the air

_____ 4. Matt's four-year-old niece caught a cold after she was **exposed to** a friend who was sick. They had shared toys and food all day.

_____ 5. The **incidence of** AIDS continues to rise in some countries. There are many new cases every year.

_____ 6. Cold viruses are **transmitted** when someone sneezes or coughs. The viruses move quickly through the air.

d. number of cases of	e. carried	f. came into contact with

_____ 7. Good nutrition and clean water are **crucial** to good health.

_____ 8. Our professor suddenly became very sick. The doctors didn't think he would **recover**, but within a week he felt much better.

_____ 9. Angela was worried about her final exam. The **stress** gave her a headache, and she couldn't sleep.

g. extremely important	h. tension	i. to get better

_____ 10. If we have adaptive immunity, our bodies are familiar with the **microorganisms** around us, and we can fight them off.

_____ 11. There are things we can do to **promote** good health, such as exercise regularly and not smoke.

_____ 12. Dr. Jin gave the man a flu **vaccine** to prevent him from getting sick.

j. help develop	k. small creatures seen only with a microscope	l. a weak form of a virus given to protect you from the virus

B. **INTERACT WITH VOCABULARY!** Work with a partner. Read the sentences in Column A and discuss the meanings of the boldfaced phrases. Then read sentences 1–5 aloud as your partner fills in the blanks in Column B. Switch roles for 6–10.

Column A	Column B
1. The germs that the Australian tourists encountered while vacationing in Hawaii were different from those **back home**.	1. The germs that the Australian tourists encountered while vacationing in Hawaii were different from those _____ **home**.
2. We develop immunity naturally **based on** where we live and what germs we're exposed to.	2. We develop immunity naturally **based** _____ where we live and what germs we're exposed to.
3. We can **develop** immunity artificially **through** vaccines.	3. We can **develop** immunity artificially _____ vaccines.
4. The childhood disease the chicken pox is **caused by** the VZV virus.	4. The childhood disease the chicken pox is **caused** _____ the VZV virus.
5. Children need to **build up resistance to** the germs around them. That's why they're sick a lot in the beginning.	5. Children need to **build** _____ **resistance** _____ the germs around them. That's why they're sick a lot in the beginning.
6. As children get older, they **tend to** get sick less.	6. As children get older, they **tend** _____ get sick less.
7. Let's take a look at adaptive immunity **in more detail**.	7. Let's take a look at adaptive immunity _____ **more detail**.
8. We all get sick **from time to time**. No one is 100 percent healthy at all times!	8. We all get sick _____ **time** _____ **time**. No one is 100 percent healthy at all times!
9. After Meg had the chicken pox, she was **immune to** it. She won't get it again.	9. After Meg had the chicken pox, she was **immune** _____ it. She won't get it again.
10. The travelers drank bottled water to **keep from getting sick**.	10. The travelers drank bottled water to **keep** _____ **getting sick**.

FOCUS *your* attention

CONNECTED IDEAS

Lecturers want you to understand how their ideas are connected. One way they do this is by pointing out a cause-and-effect relationship (A). Or a lecturer may try to help you make a connection to an idea mentioned earlier (B). For example:

> (A) If . . . , then . . .
>   Because of . . .
>   . . . This results in . . .
>
> (B) Do you recall . . .
>   Think back to . . .
>   As I mentioned earlier . . .

Sometimes, it's hard to connect ideas when a lecturer briefly talks about something else (A). But, the lecturer will often signal a return to the topic (B).

> (A) I have to add a quick
>   comment . . .
>   Before I forget . . .
>   I want to mention . . .
>
> (B) Anyway, moving on . . .
>   Back to our focus today . . .
>   Back to (the topic) . . .

You can show cause-and-effect relationships with an arrow (→) between ideas. Say you hear *If you're exposed to a virus, **then** you might get sick.* Your notes might looks like this:

exposed to a virus → might get sick

TRY IT OUT!

A. Listen to this excerpt from a public health presentation. What phrases do you hear that help you connect the ideas? Take notes.

B. Compare notes with a partner.

LISTEN *to the* lecture

BEFORE YOU LISTEN

You are about to listen to this unit's lecture on building immunity and some of the health risks of international travel. What are two risks you can think of?

_____

LISTEN FOR MAIN IDEAS

A. **Close your book. Listen to the lecture and take notes.**

B. **Use your notes. Answer the questions, based on the lecture. Circle *a*, *b*, or *c*.**

1. What's the lecture mainly about?

   a. the importance of adaptive immunity

   b. the importance of good nutrition

   c. the importance of clean water

2. Which *isn't* true of adaptive immunity?

   a. It's the ability to fight the diseases we are exposed to.

   b. It's more difficult to develop it in Beijing than in Paris.

   c. We can develop it naturally and artificially.

3. Why is the incidence of disease transmission rising?

   a. because the number of people getting vaccines has decreased

   b. because the number of people getting medical care has decreased

   c. because global travel has increased

4. What is the speaker's attitude toward vaccines?

   a. It's up to the person; they're a personal choice.

   b. They should be given to everyone.

   c. They aren't necessary if we have good food and water.

5. What does the comparison between Meg and Kimi show?

   a. that people respond differently to diseases

   b. that there are many childhood diseases

   c. that there are different types of adaptive immunity

6. What's the speaker's attitude about staying healthy?

   a. It's difficult to stay healthy.

   b. It's important to have a healthy lifestyle.

   c. It's expensive to keep people healthy.

LISTEN FOR DETAILS

A. Close your book. Listen to the lecture again. Add details to your notes and correct any mistakes.

B. Use your notes. Circle the answer that best completes the sentence, based on the lecture.

1. How healthy we are depends on how (strong / weak) our immune system is.

2. The speaker conducted research on vaccines for children in (Ecuador / Africa).

3. We develop (diseases / immunity) to the microorganisms we grow up around.

4. Children one to three years old tend to get sick (less / more).

5. Someone traveling to another country (is / isn't) protected by the adaptive immunity they developed back home.

6. The speaker mentions (AIDS / avian flu) as an example of a contagious disease that public health officials are concerned about.

7. Someone who gets a cold probably (will / won't) get one again because there are many cold viruses.

8. Someone who gets the chicken pox (will / won't) normally get it again because his or her body now has an immunological memory of it.

9. The idea behind vaccines is that it's better to (treat sick people / keep people from getting sick).

10. (Stress / Reducing stress) can lower our immunity.

TALK *about the* topic

A. Listen to the students talk about building immunity. Read each comment. Then check (✓) the student who makes the comment.

		Michael	Yhinny	Qiang	May
1.	"Well, last year, I was on this study abroad program where you travel around the world by ship . . . "	☐	☐	☐	☐
2.	"So, your body didn't learn to adapt to the germs, huh?"	☐	☐	☐	☐
3.	"Wow, the lecturer would not agree with that decision!"	☐	☐	☐	☐
4.	"And, I should tell you all—I'm a total clean freak!"	☐	☐	☐	☐

Michael

Yhinny

Qiang

May

B. Listen to the discussion again. Listen closely for the comments below. Check (✓) the discussion strategy the student uses.

		Asking for opinions or ideas	Offering a fact or example	Paraphrasing
1.	**Michael:** "So, I can tell you from personal experience about the importance of adaptive immunity."	☐	☐	☐
2.	**Yhinny:** "She said it can take your body two years to learn to fight off some microorganisms."	☐	☐	☐
3.	**May:** "What about your diet?"	☐	☐	☐
4.	**Michael:** "But, anyways, what about everyone else?"	☐	☐	☐

Discussion Strategy: By **offering a fact or example**, you can transform a topic from theory to reality. This can make the topic not only more understandable, but also more memorable. Personal experiences ("In my experience . . ."), observations ("I've noticed . . .") and media ("I just read this artice in the *Times* . . .") are a few ways you can begin.

C. In small groups, discuss one or more of these topics. Try to use the discussion strategies you have learned.

- Have you had any health problems while you were traveling?
- Michael mentions that it was stressful to travel. Do you think it is?
- Yhinny's parents are against vaccines. Do you agree with them?

REVIEW *your* notes

Work with a partner. Use your notes. Retell these main ideas in your own words.

- What immunity is and why we need it
- What we mean by both "natural" and "artificial" adaptive immunity
- Why traveling can make it more difficult to stay healthy
- How vaccines work
- The main difference between Kimi's and Meg's illnesses:

  If Kimi gets exposed to a cold virus again, she …
  Meg is exposed to chicken pox again, but she doesn't get sick because of …

Complete these notes. Connect the ideas, focusing on cause-and-effect relationships.

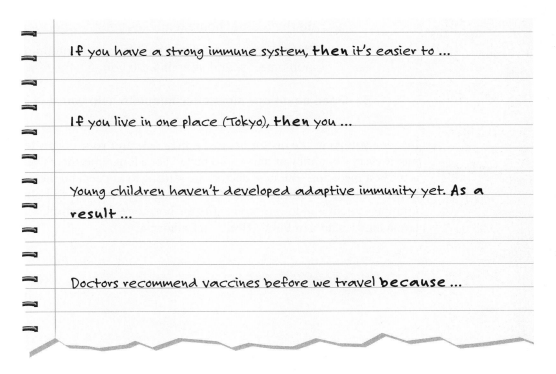

If you have a strong immune system, **then** it's easier to …

If you live in one place (Tokyo), **then** you …

Young children haven't developed adaptive immunity yet. **As a result** …

Doctors recommend vaccines before we travel **because** …

TAKE THE UNIT TEST

Now you are ready to take the Unit Test.

> **Tip!**
>
> Remember to listen for and use cause-and-effect signals like these:
> If . . . then . . .
> . . . as a result . . .
> . . . because . . .

EXTEND *the* topic

Everyone wants to stay healthy, of course. But getting sick now and then is natural. Listen and read about comforting yourself when you are sick, and some practices that can help you stay well.

 A. **Listen to a radio talk show host interview a doctor about what helps us recover when we are sick. Discuss these questions with your classmates.**

1. Do you have "comfort foods"—foods you like to eat when you're sick?

2. Are there other home remedies you try when you have a cold?

3. There are many products sold to boost immunity: energy drinks, herbal supplements, and vitamins. Do you use these when you have a cold?

B. **Read about one simple technique to help you stay healthy.**

Imagine you go to the doctor because you're sick, and your doctor tells you to watch a comedy movie every day until you start to feel better! For a long time, there's been the expression "laughter is the best medicine." But now doctors are starting to understand the power of laughing. In fact, in England there's an official Laugh Clinic. Laughing makes us feel good. It also strengthens the immune system and lowers levels of stress hormones like cortisol, according to Dr. Lee Bark of Loma Linda School of Public Health in California.

"I'd say you're not eating right."

Laughing is also good exercise. It fills the lungs with oxygen and gives the heart a workout. Researchers studied heart attack patients. Patients who spent thirty minutes a day watching comedy videos had a 10 percent chance of a second heart attack, compared with a 30 percent chance if they didn't laugh each day. Watching a sitcom or a few video clips on a comedy website at the end of a stressful day may be a good way to stay healthy!

Work with a partner. Answer these questions.

1. What do you do to have fun and relax?

2. What makes you laugh?

3. Do you have a favorite comedy movie you would recommend to a friend?

C. Research one of the following topics. Prepare a presentation for the class or small group.

- - - -> Go to the Centers for Disease Control website (www.cdc.gov/). Research general tips on traveling abroad. Then choose a country to visit. Find out the travel recommendations for vaccines as well as tips regarding food, water, and other safety issues.

- - - -> Public health involves many fields, such as biology, mathematics, engineering, computer science, medicine, psychology, and anthropology. Search the Internet using the keywords *public health jobs* to find out about career possibilities within public health.

UNIT 10

Principles of Journalism

CONNECT *to the* topic

How do you find out what's going on? We're surrounded by media options: books, radio, film, TV, newspapers, magazines, the Internet, podcasts, YouTube, Facebook, and on and on. Every day, huge amounts of information are transmitted to all of us. What's the best way to get the news you want and trust? Electronic media are developing rapidly and are becoming increasingly easy to access. As news sources continue to evolve, so do the discussions about journalism and the principles guiding those who report the news to us.

Take this survey about media habits. Circle or write in your answers.

········➤ How important is it to know what's going on in the world?

    not very   somewhat   very

········➤ Which kinds of news do you follow?

    sports   fashion   politics   business   entertainment   friends   other

········➤ Which media do you use for news/information?

    books   radio   film   TV   newspapers   magazines   the Internet

········➤ How often do you get news?

    every day   2–3 times a week   less than once a week

········➤ Do you like to read or write blogs?

    Yes, I like to read/write about _____.   No.

········➤ How often is news fair and accurate?

    most of the time   some of the time   never

Compare responses with a partner.

BUILD *your* vocabulary

 A. **The boldfaced words are from this unit's lecture on journalism. Listen to each sentence. Then circle the meaning of the boldfaced word.**

1. There was a big fire. In order to cover the story **adequately**, the reporter talked to many people and was able to verify that the information she had was accurate.

   enough for a particular purpose   very quickly   bravely

2. Principles of good journalism were **compiled** by a committee of journalists. They gathered ideas from thousands of journalists around the world.

   pressed down   put together from different sources   discussed

3. Many TV reporters **covered** the World Cup; you could find broadcasts on every station.

   reported the details of a news event   protected   were interested in

4. The reporter had strong **ethics**. When her coworker told her that he'd made up part of a news story to make it more interesting, she told the manager.

   opinions   job background   rules about what is right and wrong

5. There are **multiple** places to find out what's going on: TV, radio, the Internet, newspapers, and so on.

   ordinary   many   official

6. Alberto was an **objective** reporter. His story included only facts about the crime, not his opinion of who did it.

   stubborn   not influenced by one's own beliefs   observant

7. Journalists have an **obligation** to keep the public informed about what the government does; that's their job.

   the process of watching someone   duty   right

8. A new **paradigm** for journalism is developing as more and more people use electronic media to get their news.

   importance   model or approach   rule

9. We can stay informed by following both **professional** journalists and ordinary citizens who write blogs.

   hardworking   dependable   trained to do a job for money

10. The **underlying** principles of good journalism are the same for newspapers, magazines, Internet news sites, and blogs.

    not desirable   basic, fundamental   inconvenient

B. Now complete each sentence with the correct word.

compiled	ethic	obligation	profession	underlying

1. A(n) _____ principle of journalism is to tell the truth. It's a

    basic _____ of the _____ .

2. Journalists have a(n) _____ to know what's going on.

3. The news story was _____ by two reporters.

adequate	cover	multiple	objective	paradigm

4. There's a new _____ in the field of journalism. Think about

    how reporters _____ stories now.

5. Talking to only one person isn't _____ . Journalists should use

    _____ sources for a news story.

6. Readers don't want opinions. They want _____ information.

C. *INTERACT WITH VOCABULARY!* Work in pairs. Notice the boldfaced words. Read sentence starters 1–5 as your partner chooses the phrase that completes the sentence. Switch roles for 6–10.

1. For a deep **understanding** . . .   a. **of** local issues, read your local paper.

2. Stories should offer a **balance** . . .   b. **of media,** including radio and TV.

3. The reporter interviewed **multiple** . . . c. **of** views, not just one source.

4. There are different **kinds** . . .   d. **sources:** a victim, a cop, and a witness.

5. *Wire stories* are **compiled** . . .   e. **by** the Associated Press, for example.

6. Some websites are **extensions** . . .   f. **to** their audience.

7. International journalists **report** . . .   g. **of** news. They're not professionals.

8. Bloggers write their own **version** . . .   h. **of** TV networks, like CNN.com.

9. News stories shouldn't be **biased** . . .   i. **toward** one point of view.

10. Editors choose stories **relevant** . . .   j. **on** world issues.

FOCUS *your* attention

LECTURE ORGANIZATION

One way speakers can indicate lecture organization is by enumerating and repeating key phrases. For example:

> *Today I'm going to talk about* **three characteristics of a good news website***.*
>
> *I'm going to present* **seven principles of good journalism***.*
>
> *I'm going to focus on* **four reasons some people prefer the Internet as their news source***.*

A speaker will present one characteristic, principle, or reason at a time, and then will indicate what's next by **stating a new number** and **repeating the key phrase** (A). Speakers also often let you know when a topic is finished (B).

> *(A)* **Characteristic 1: A good news website** *provides accurate information . . .*
>
> **Characteristic 2: A good news website** *has many types of stories: sports, politics, . . .*
>
> *(B)* **Now I want to turn to . . .**   **Moving on now to . . .**
>   **Let's now look at . . .**

These notes are from a lecture organized with key phrases and numbers.

A good news website	
Characteristics	Examples / details
1) provides accurate information	checks facts ...
2) has many types of stories	sports, politics ...

TRY IT OUT!

A. **Listen to this excerpt from a journalism class. What key phrases and numbers do you hear? Take notes in a chart.**

B. **Compare notes with a partner.**

LISTEN *to the* lecture

BEFORE YOU LISTEN

You are about to listen to this unit's lecture on journalistic principles. In your opinion, what makes someone a good journalist?

_____

LISTEN FOR MAIN IDEAS

A. **Close your book. Listen to the lecture and take notes.**

B. **Use your notes. Answer the questions, based on the lecture. Circle *a*, *b*, or *c*.**

1. What topic does the lecturer talk about first?

    a. the characteristics of a good newspaper

    b. the advantages of different media sources

    c. the underlying principles of good journalism

2. Which of the following ideas does the speaker mainly discuss?
   Circle TWO answers.

    a. Journalists need to be objective.

    b. Journalists need to become better writers.

    c. Journalists need to tell the truth.

3. What is the second part of the lecture mainly about?

    a. the impact of the Internet on traditional journalism

    b. the increase in the types of electronic media

    c. the reasons for an increase in electronic media

4. What does the speaker think about blogs?

    a. They hurt professional journalism.

    b. They should follow the principles of professional journalism.

    c. They should be controlled more by the government.

5. What does the speaker think will happen to journalism in the future?

    a. that it will be more difficult to get a job as a journalist

    b. that the field of journalism will eventually die out, like the dinosaurs

    c. that a new relationship will develop between bloggers and professional journalists

LISTEN FOR DETAILS

A. **Close your book. Listen to the lecture again. Add details to your notes and correct any mistakes.**

B. **Use your notes. Circle the word that best completes each idea, according to the lecture.**

1. The Committee of Concerned Journalists spent (five / seven) years conducting their research.

2. The speaker says the principles of good journalism apply to (newspaper journalists / all media).

3. The main point of Principle 1 is that the public expects journalists to (judge what news to trust / tell the truth).

4. Principle 2 is that journalists' first obligation is to (the owners of the news media / the public).

5. Principle 4, "be a watchdog," means journalists need to keep people informed about what (the government / the public) is doing.

6. The main point of Principle 5 is that journalists need to report relevant news in an (interesting / objective) way.

7. According to Principle 7, the public needs to get (all sides of a story / a complete picture of what's going on in their community).

8. Today more journalists gather information (in their offices / at the scene of an event) than in the past.

9. Internet news sites (have / have not) significantly increased the number of news outlets because many are owned by other media, such as TV networks.

10. "Citizen journalists" are ordinary people who write (blogs / news stories for local newspapers).

TALK *about the* topic

A. Listen to the students talk about journalism. Read each idea.
Then check (☑) the student who agrees with it.

	Molly	Rob	Alana	Ayman
1. Journalism is about reporting facts.	☐	☐	☐	☐
2. A good journalist should be able to tell a story well.	☐	☐	☐	☐
3. Balance can be found by going to a variety of media, such as radio, the Internet, and magazines.	☐	☐	☐	☐
4. Blogs often present a different point of view than traditional media.	☐	☐	☐	☐

B. Listen to the discussion again. Listen closely for the comments below.
Check (☑) the discussion strategy the student uses.

	Expressing an opinion	Agreeing	Paraphrasing
1. **Molly:** "What she means is she has the talent for making something interesting."	☐	☐	☐
2. **Alana:** "Yeah, exactly."	☐	☐	☐
3. **Alana:** "Even some 'journalists' don't tell the whole truth."	☐	☐	☐
4. **Molly:** "Hello! Now *those* are the real storytellers!"	☐	☐	☐
5. **Rob:** "Tell me about it!"	☐	☐	☐

> **Discussion Strategy:** When you **paraphrase**, you restate in your own words
> something that someone else has said or written. Here are some common ways of
> introducing paraphrased ideas: "What she meant was . . ."; "In other words . . .";
> "His point was . . ."; "She basically said . . . ."

C. In small groups, discuss one or more of these topics. Try to use the discussion
strategies you have learned.

- Do you have any favorite news columns or news blogs? What do you like about them?
- Why is it important for a journalist to be a good storyteller? What other qualities are important?
- Alana mentions journalists on political channels, and Molly responds, "Now *those* are the real storytellers!" What does she mean by this?

REVIEW *your* notes

In the lecture, the speaker presents good journalism from the point of view of the Committee of Concerned Journalists. She uses phrases such as *journalists need to* and *journalists must*. Work with a partner. Compare the following statements:

> *Journalists often use several sources.* (a fact)

> *Journalists need to use several sources.* (point of view)

Next in the lecture, the speaker discusses the impact of the Internet. Compare the following statements:

> *Many reporters rarely leave their offices.* (fact)

> *I don't think professional journalists will become extinct, like dinosaurs.* (point of view)

Using your notes, discuss both the facts and the points of view/opinions presented in the lecture. Be sure to cover the topics below. Then complete the notes.

---

7 principles from Committee of Concerned Journalists:

1)   5)

2)   6)

3)   7)

4)

Impact of Internet on journalism:

citizen journalists vs. professional journalists:

Speaker's point of view about future of journalism:

Now you are ready to take the Unit Test.

E X T E N D *the* topic

> *Have you read or listened to any news today? Has studying journalistic principles changed how you receive the news you get? You can expand your understanding of current media trends with the following activities.*

A. Listen to owners of a local paper appeal for help at a city council meeting. Discuss these questions with your classmates.

1. Would it matter to you if traditional hard-copy newspapers no longer existed?

2. Is there a local newspaper in your hometown?

3. Some people say a local newspaper provides an important social network for people in a community. Do you agree?

B. Read about one type of journalism that has no problem drawing readers.

Journalists' first obligation is to the public, not to advertisers or the owners of the news media. However, for the owners it's a business. They want to make money, and they know some stories will attract people more than others. Increasingly, they have found that celebrity gossip attracts a lot of people! Celebrity journalism focuses on the personal lives of actors, artists, musicians, models, athletes, and anyone else in the spotlight who ordinary people want to know about. What celebrities wear, who they marry and divorce, what they name their babies, where they vacation, even what they like to snack on are all "must-know news" for many people.

Rupert Murdoch, chairman and CEO of News Corporation, understands this very well. On "Page 6" of the *New York Post*, a tabloid newspaper Murdoch owns, readers can find fresh celebrity gossip. News outlets know that some stories "sell" better than others, and celebrity gossip sells well.

Work with a partner to answer these questions.

1. Do you like to read celebrity news? Where do you get it?

2. Should media outlets increase celebrity news if this is what people want?

3. Is it important to balance celebrity news and other types of news?

C. **Research one of these journalism topics.**

····> Choose a story currently in the news. Gather information using at least three media sources such as TV, newspapers, and Internet news sites including blogs. Pay attention to any differences in how the news story is reported. Prepare a short, balanced summary.

····> Choose a personal community website from any country and show how people exchange news and opinions via these communities. Prepare a short presentation.

UNIT 11

DNA Testing

"Your DNA test shows a weakness for pasta with extra cheese."

CONNECT *to the* topic

To explain a "weakness," we sometimes say, "It's in my DNA!" meaning it's just who we are—we can't help it. DNA is a substance inside each cell of our body. It contains genetic information from our parents and determines our appearance, talents, and even what diseases we may develop. We each have our own set of DNA, called our genome. This makes each of us unique. Scientists can now identify an organism just by examining its genome—by testing the DNA. This discovery has sparked an explosion of possibilities in the field of biotechnology.

Describe yourself in the chart below. Then complete the information about your family. Who in your family do you resemble?

	You	Mother	Father	Sister or Brother
eye color				
hair color				
height				
personality				
talents				
diseases				

Discuss with a partner.

BUILD *your* vocabulary

A. **The boldfaced words are from this unit's lecture on DNA testing. Listen to each sentence. Then guess the meaning of the boldfaced word.**

1. The police wanted **access to** DNA samples taken from the suspect. But the judge refused to release the samples.

2. The researchers **concentrated on** the role genetics play in our health. They didn't focus on anything else.

3. Dr. Hassan couldn't figure out what was wrong with her patient. She decided to use genetic testing to help **diagnose** the patient's disease.

4. In the crime lab, scientists **extract** DNA from samples of hair, skin, and fingernails. After they remove the DNA from the samples, they test it.

5. The twin brothers looked a lot alike, but they weren't **identical** twins; one had brown hair and one had blond hair.

6. The lab technician saw that the two blood samples didn't **match**, so she concluded that the blood was from two different people.

7. The **medical** field uses DNA tests to find out who is at risk for certain diseases.

8. The Morettis wanted to have a baby, so they had a DNA test. It **revealed** that their baby might inherit a genetic disorder from the father.

9. **Statistically**, it's very unlikely that two people will have the same DNA profile. The chance of this happening is less than 1 percent.

10. Our DNA contains genetic information such as eye color and other **traits** passed down from a mother and father to their child.

B. **Now complete each sentence with the correct word or phrase.**

extract	matched	medical	reveal	statistically

1. DNA research has had a big impact on the _____ field, particularly on how doctors work with their patients.

2. The lab results showed that the hair found in the suspect's car _____ the hair of the victim's cat.

3. DNA testing may _____ that something isn't normal in a person's genes. For example, it may show a person is at risk for a disease.

4. It's unlikely _____ for two DNA fingerprints to be the same.

5. To create a DNA fingerprint, scientists _____ DNA from samples taken from various parts of the body.

access to	concentrated on	diagnose	identical	trait

6. It took doctors a year to _____ the baby's disease.

7. Height is just one _____ children inherit from parents.

8. The lab workers _____ identifying the murder victim.

9. These two fingerprints aren't _____; they're different.

10. The company had _____ employees' personal information.

C. *INTERACTIVE WITH VOCABULARY!* **Work with a partner. Read the sentences in Column A and discuss the meanings of the boldfaced phrases. Then read sentences 1–5 aloud as your partner fills in the blanks in Column B. Switch roles for 6–10.**

Column A	Column B
1. The evidence **at the crime scene** was a strand of hair.	1. The evidence _____ **the crime scene** was a strand of hair.
2. Everyone has a **combination of** genetic traits from their parents.	2. Everyone has a **combination** _____ genetic traits from their parents.
3. Two sisters may **end up with** the same eye color.	3. Two sisters may **end** _____ _____ the same eye color.
4. There was a **match between** the two DNA samples.	4. There was a **match** _____ the two DNA samples.
5. A probe is a tool **used by** scientists in DNA testing.	5. A probe is a tool **used** _____ scientists in DNA testing.
6. The test showed that the woman was **at risk for** Alzheimer's disease.	6. The test showed that the woman was _____ **risk** _____ Alzheimer's disease.
7. With DNA testing come **concerns about** privacy.	7. With DNA testing come **concerns** _____ privacy.
8. Doctors give DNA tests **for one of two reasons**.	8. Doctors give DNA tests _____ **one** _____ **two reasons**.
9. Some diseases are **linked to** our genes.	9. Some diseases are **linked** _____ our genes.
10. What are the **pros and cons of** DNA testing?	10. What are the **pros** _____ **cons** _____ DNA testing?

FOCUS *your* attention

GRAPHIC ORGANIZERS

Sometimes, a lecturer presents a lot of technical information or details—for example, in describing a process. A graphic organizer is one way to help you link and remember information. You can fill in information as you listen and then add more later when you review your notes.

A speaker often uses the following signal words when describing a process. When you hear these words, move on to the next part of your organizer, as shown below.

> *They start by . . . / First . . .   After that . . .*
>
> *Next . . .   And then . . . / At that point . . .*
>
> *Then . . .   Finally . . .*

Your notes might look like this:

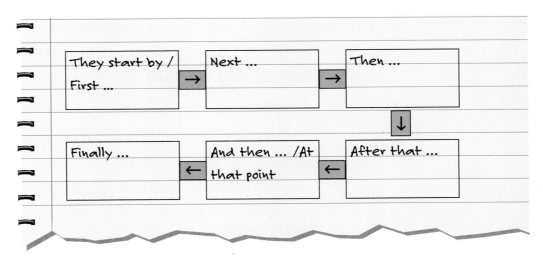

TRY IT OUT!

A. Listen to this excerpt from a crime investigation seminar. What words and phrases do you hear that signal the process? Take notes.

B. Compare notes with a partner.

LISTEN *to the* lecture

BEFORE YOU LISTEN

You are about to hear this unit's lecture on some uses of DNA testing. What uses do you know of? Write your ideas.

_____

LISTEN FOR MAIN IDEAS

A. Close your book. Listen to the lecture and take notes.

B. Use your notes. Answer the questions, based on the lecture. Circle *a*, *b,* or *c*.

1. What is the lecture mainly about?

    a. how doctors use DNA testing to cure diseases

    b. how to create a DNA fingerprint and some uses

    c. types of genetic disorders that cause diseases

2. In what order does the speaker present the topics?

    a. medical uses, privacy concerns, creating a DNA fingerprint

    b. creating a DNA fingerprint, privacy concerns, medical uses

    c. creating a DNA fingerprint, medical uses, privacy concerns

3. What is DNA fingerprinting? Choose TWO answers.

    a. making a copy of a person's DNA

    b. creating a set of data about someone using DNA

    c. creating an "ID" of someone using DNA samples from different parts of the body

4. What's one way a crime lab can use DNA testing?

    a. to identify a car accident victim

    b. to look for DNA matches between a suspect and evidence from a crime scene

    c. to let the police know there was a crime

5. What is the connection between genetic disorders and disease?

    a. Genetic disorders increase the risk of getting a disease.

    b. Scientists know genetic disorders always cause diseases.

    c. Scientists don't know if there's a link between genetic disorders and diseases.

6. What is the speaker's general attitude toward DNA testing?

    a. DNA testing is very beneficial.

    b. There are privacy issues we need to consider.

    c. DNA testing should be done more often.

LISTEN FOR DETAILS

A. **Close your book. Listen to the lecture again. Add details to your notes and correct any mistakes.**

B. **Use your notes. Decide if the statements below are true (*T*) or false (*F*), according to the lecture. Correct the false statements.**

____ 1. Another way to say "DNA fingerprint" is "DNA profile."

____ 2. The speaker thinks it's statistically likely that a brother and sister will have identical genetic information.

____ 3. DNA testing proved that Marie Antoinette's son escaped from prison.

____ 4. A crime lab uses probes to see if DNA samples from a suspect match DNA samples from evidence at a crime scene.

____ 5. The more probes that match, the stronger the case against the suspect's.

____ 6. Scientists have found that DNA identification in a crime lab is 100 percent foolproof.

____ 7. According to the speaker, there are more than 16,000 genetic disorders.

____ 8. The speaker says that a mutation—a change in a gene—will definitely cause a disease.

____ 9. The speaker says that one benefit of DNA testing is that it might save someone's life.

____ 10. The speaker is concerned about who should have access to someone's DNA profile.

TALK *about the* topic

A. Listen to the students talk about DNA testing. Read each opinion. Then check (✓) who agrees with it.

	Hannah	River	Manny	Mia
1. Doctors and the government already have all other personal information.	☐	☐	☐	☐
2. If I have a DNA test, it's nobody's business but my own.	☐	☐	☐	☐
3. DNA is good information for the police to have access to, like in the example of crime.	☐	☐	☐	☐
4. DNA results that show risk for disease just cause worry.	☐	☐	☐	☐

B. Listen to the discussion again. Listen closely for the comments below. Check (✓) the discussion strategy the student uses.

	Expressing an opinion	Disagreeing	Keeping the discussion on topic
1. **River:** "Yeah, isn't she great?"	☐	☐	☐
2. **Hannah:** "Sorry, guys … That's not really why we're here. We're supposed to … "	☐	☐	☐
3. **Manny:** "Come on. That's not true."	☐	☐	☐
4. **Hannah:** "Hey … back to DNA, OK?"	☐	☐	☐
5. **Mia:** "I think we're all going to worry about something."	☐	☐	☐

C. In small groups, discuss one or more of these topics. Try to use the discussion strategies you have learned.

- Do you agree that the results of your DNA test are nobody else's business?
- Is it ever good for others to have access to your DNA information?
- Have you heard of people being freed from prison because of DNA testing? If so, what were the details?

REVIEW *your* notes

Use your notes. Work with a partner to complete the organizer and answer the questions below. Then retell the main ideas of the lecture in your own words.

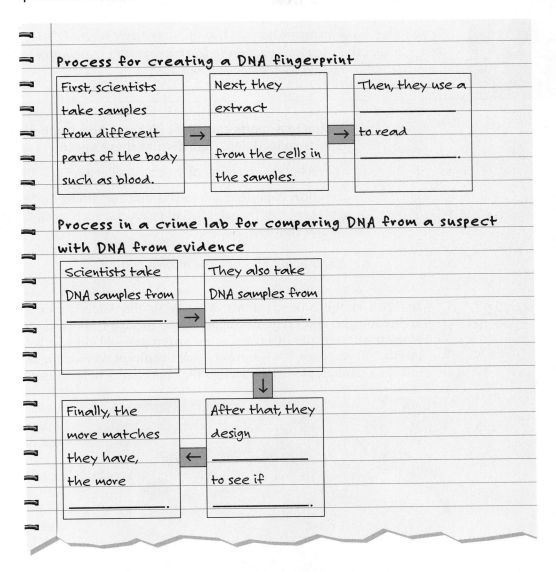

Process for creating a DNA fingerprint

First, scientists take samples from different parts of the body such as blood. → Next, they extract _____ from the cells in the samples. → Then, they use a _____ to read _____.

Process in a crime lab for comparing DNA from a suspect with DNA from evidence

Scientists take DNA samples from _____. → They also take DNA samples from _____. ↓

Finally, the more matches they have, the more _____. ← After that, they design _____ to see if _____.

- What two medical uses of DNA testing are mentioned?
- What is the relationship between genetic disorders and diseases?
- What are the pros and cons of DNA testing in medicine?
- What privacy questions does the speaker consider?

TAKE THE UNIT TEST

Now you are ready to take the Unit Test.

▪▪▪ EXTEND *the* topic

Criminology and medicine are just two of many fields where DNA testing is useful. Listen and read on to learn about other fascinating ways that DNA-related technology is being used.

A. **Listen to a sports collector talk about how synthetic DNA is used to mark sports collectibles. Then discuss these questions with your classmates.**

1. What do you think of "serious collectors"?

2. How important is it to you that something be "authentic"? Do you ever buy "knock-offs" of products, such as designer shoes, handbags, or clothes?

B. **Read about another use of DNA testing.**

In 1995, at the summit of Mt. Ampato in the Andes Mountains, Johan Reinhard, an anthropologist, and his guide Miguel Zarate made a fantastic discovery. They found the Ice Maiden—the remains of a twelve- to fourteen-year-old girl who had been sacrificed by Incan priests 500 years ago. This discovery was significant because the body was frozen, not dried out. As a result, it provided scientists the opportunity to learn new information about Incan

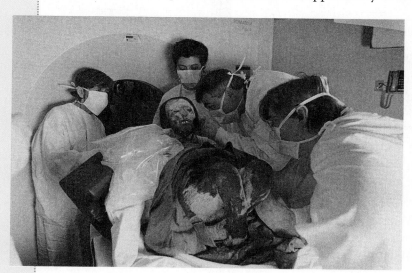

life. For example, the scientists could test the girl's body tissue to learn about the Incan health and diet. They could study her colorful, frozen clothing and learn about the materials used. And they could extract DNA to study the girl's genetic origin, and possibly learn about her family. They could even possibly map a genetic path to her relatives still living today.

The Ice Maiden

Discuss these questions with a partner.

1. Anthropologists use DNA testing to study family lineage. What do you know about your family's background? Consider the cities, countries, and regions where family members lived or currently live.

2. DNA testing is used to find out if certain genetic disorders run in families. Suppose there were a medical database with information about your family, including relatives from the past. What would you want to know?

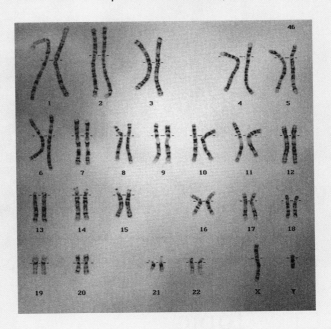

C. **Choose one of the following topics to research. Prepare a short presentation for the class or a small group.**

---> The Innocence Project: a project that uses DNA testing to free prison inmates held for crimes they didn't commit

---> The Frozen Ark Project: a project that stores DNA and tissue samples of endangered animals worldwide

---> Other DNA testing uses:
  - officials who "tag" food items, such as fish or caviar, to authenticate the item
  - hospitals that search for organ donors for sick patients
  - coroners who identify victims of earthquakes or other natural disasters
  - children who want to determine their biological parents
  - pet owners who want to know their pets' background
  - parents-to-be who want to know more about an egg or sperm donor

UNIT 12

Risk Management

CONNECT *to the* topic

We know we can't control nature. There are many natural hazards, including tornados, hurricanes, earthquakes, and tsunamis. But we do know that we can prepare for them so that they don't automatically become disasters.

Work with a partner. Discuss these questions about natural disasters.

⟫ Have you experienced a tornado, hurricane, earthquake, or tsunami? If so, what happened?

⟫ What natural disasters have you heard about recently?

⟫ What seem to be the three biggest problems for people after a natural disaster?

⟫ How important do you think emergency plans are?

⟫ Imagine there is a natural disaster and you have to leave your home. You have only five minutes to decide what to take with you. What do you take? Why?

BUILD *your* vocabulary

A. The boldfaced words below are from this unit's lecture on emergency planning. Listen to each sentence. Then match the meaning to the boldfaced word.

____ 1. The government will **allocate** part of its budget for roads, but it also needs to budget money for schools.

____ 2. After a natural disaster, people should **cooperate** by doing what the officials ask.

____ 3. It's important to **minimize** the impact of hurricanes. We can reduce the damage by being prepared.

      a. to do what someone is asked to do
      b. to make the amount of something as small as possible
      c. to decide to allow a certain amount of money to be used

____ 4. Sometimes, people **ignore** government orders to evacuate. They don't listen to instructions to leave, even though it might be dangerous to stay home.

____ 5. Experts can't **predict** exactly when an earthquake will occur.

____ 6. Governments set spending **priorities**. What's needed more: better health care or more public transportation?

____ 7. The Gulf Coast region of the United States is disaster-**prone**; in other words, a disaster is more likely to occur there than in some other parts of the country.

      a. likely to do something or to suffer from something
      b. to say that something will happen before it happens
      c. the things that are most important and need attention first
      d. to refuse to pay attention to

____ 8. Our local public safety officer held an informational meeting about what to do during a tornado in hopes of **mitigating** the townspeople's fears.

____ 9. Educational programs **targeted** at students help them understand the risks of local natural hazards.

____ 10. It's difficult for every citizen to be totally prepared for a natural disaster. **Ultimately**, it's up to the government to try its best to keep people safe.

____ 11. The hurricane caused **widespread** damage: Houses were destroyed throughout the region.

      a. in the end
      b. happening in many places or situations or with many people
      c. aimed at, developed for
      d. making less severe, not as bad

B. *INTERACT WITH VOCABULARY!* **Work with a partner. Read the sentences in Column A and discuss the meanings of the boldfaced phrases. Then read sentences 1–4 aloud as your partner fills in the blanks in Column B. Switch roles for 5–8.**

Column A	Column B
1. Small earthquakes usually don't cause damage. **By the same token**, there are always exceptions.	1. Small earthquakes usually don't cause damage. _____ **the same token**, there are always exceptions.
2. Fortunately, the hurricane **died out** and caused no problems.	2. Fortunately, the hurricane **died** _____ and caused no problems.
3. Let's look at some factors **involved in** generating an emergency plan.	3. Let's look at some factors **involved** _____ generating an emergency plan.
4. Experts can't **predict with 100 percent accuracy**. They don't know for sure when a storm will hit.	4. Experts can't **predict** _____ **100 percent accuracy**. They don't know for sure when a storm will hit.
5. Preparedness is **the state of being ready**.	5. Preparedness is **the state** _____ **being ready**.
6. The government needs to establish a **channel of communication** with scientists.	6. The government needs to establish a **channel** _____ **communication** with scientists.
7. The government had a strong emergency plan **in place** in many cities. They were well prepared.	7. The government had a strong emergency plan _____ **place** in many cities. They were well prepared.
8. **The logic behind** the UNESCO program is that educating children will benefit everyone.	8. **The logic** _____ the UNESCO program is that educating children will benefit everyone.

FOCUS *your* attention

QUESTIONS

As you listen to a lecture, you may not quite understand what the speaker says, or you may simply want to know more. You can write a question mark (?) in the margin of your notes to help you keep track of the questions you have. Sometimes, you're lucky and the speaker answers your question later on in the lecture. But other times you'll need to find the answer yourself after class.

Say the speaker mentions Hurricane Katrina, but you miss the year it happened. Later, the speaker says *As I mentioned, Hurricane Katrina was in 2005*. You can quickly write down the date, draw an arrow up, and continue taking notes. Then, when you review your notes, you can make revisions. Your notes might look like this:

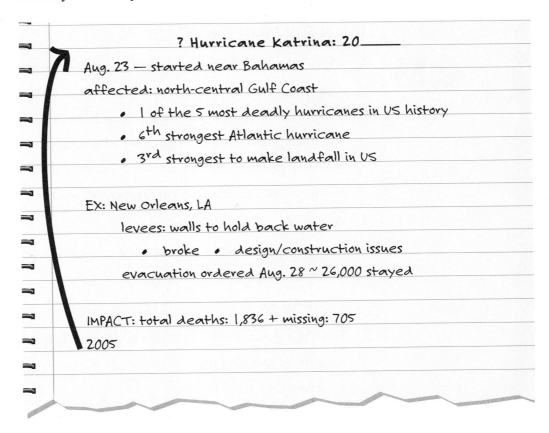

> **? Hurricane Katrina: 20____**
>
> Aug. 23 — started near Bahamas
> affected: north-central Gulf Coast
> - 1 of the 5 most deadly hurricanes in US history
> - 6th strongest Atlantic hurricane
> - 3rd strongest to make landfall in US
>
> EX: New Orleans, LA
>   levees: walls to hold back water
>   - broke   - design/construction issues
>   evacuation ordered Aug. 28 ~ 26,000 stayed
>
> IMPACT: total deaths: 1,836 + missing: 705
> 2005

TRY IT OUT!

A. Listen to this excerpt from a conference on emergency planning. Take notes. Write a question mark (?) in your notes if you miss information. Use arrows if you hear it later or get it from another student.

B. What questions do you have? Compare notes with a partner.

LISTEN *to the* lecture

BEFORE YOU LISTEN

You are about to listen to a public administration lecture about emergency planning. What are important considerations for a government? Rank these considerations from 1 to 6, with 1 being most important.

____ buy food, blankets, emergency supplies

____ train emergency workers

____ tell the public what the emergency plan is

____ have temporary housing ready

____ give emergency cell phones to every household

____ build emergency animal shelters for pets

LISTEN FOR MAIN IDEAS

A. **Close your book. Listen to the lecture and take notes.**

B. **Use your notes. Answer the questions, based on the lecture. Circle *a*, *b*, or *c*.**

1. Why does the speaker compare natural hazards and natural disasters?

    a. to emphasize the different types of natural disasters

    b. to emphasize that they are not the same thing

    c. to emphasize that they can happen anywhere

2. What is the main point of the lecture?

    a. that it's possible to prevent some natural disasters

    b. that emergency plans are vital

    c. both *a* and *b*

3. What is a government's first step in developing an emergency plan?

    a. setting spending priorities

    b. evaluating services

    c. identifying the natural hazards it faces

4. What is one of the biggest challenges for governments and scientists?

    a. organizing emergency supplies

    b. knowing what to tell the public and when

    c. trying to control natural hazards

5. What is the speaker's main point about Hurricane Katrina and the public?

    a. Many services are needed.

    b. Information isn't useful if it's ignored.

    c. It hit New Orleans.

6. What seems to be the speaker's attitude toward the UNESCO program?

    a. It shouldn't be a spending priority.

    b. It's a very positive step.

    c. It's not an essential part of emergency preparation.

LISTEN FOR DETAILS

A. Close your book. Listen to the lecture again. Add details to your notes and correct any mistakes.

B. Use your notes. Decide if the statements below are *T* (true) or *F* (false), according to the lecture. Correct the false statements.

____ 1. A natural hazard means there is the potential for a lot of damage.

____ 2. The speaker mentions the earthquake in Pakistan in 2005 as an example of a terrible disaster.

____ 3. Disaster mitigation means preparing for a natural disaster so that people will suffer less.

____ 4. The speaker mentions earthquakes and typhoons as examples of natural hazards in the United States.

____ 5. If scientists predict incorrectly, the public may not be willing to cooperate in the future.

____ 6. Sixty-one percent of the people in New Orleans didn't evacuate because they didn't want to leave.

____ 7. The fourth factor in an emergency plan includes determining if there are enough trained emergency workers.

____ 8. Setting spending priorities is difficult because governments know natural disasters always happen.

____ 9. The main goal of the UNESCO program is to make just children safer.

____ 10. The speaker mentions Turkey, Japan, and Cuba as countries where UNESCO safety programs have been successful.

TALK *about the* topic

A. Listen to the students talk about natural disasters. Read each idea. Then check (☑) the student who agrees with it.

		Alana	Rob	Molly	Ayman
1.	Nature can be dangerous, but it's not always destructive.	☐	☐	☐	☐
2.	People have a responsibility to stay safe.	☐	☐	☐	☐
3.	Money is probably a big reason that hazards become disasters.	☐	☐	☐	☐
4.	Safety education is priceless.	☐	☐	☐	☐

B. Listen to the discussion again. Listen closely for the comments below. Check (☑) the discussion strategy or strategies the student uses.

		Asking for opinions or ideas	Agreeing	Offering a fact or example
1.	**Ayman:** "So, what did you guys think of the lecture?"	☐	☐	☐
2.	**Molly:** "Yeah, not only that, but it also … "	☐	☐	☐
3.	**Molly:** "Like with Hurricane Katrina in the U.S. back in 2005?"	☐	☐	☐
4.	**Ayman:** "Like look at earthquakes— how can someone be responsible for something so unexpected?"	☐	☐	☐
5.	**Molly:** "Education, like the UNESCO program, is one inexpensive way to make a really big difference."	☐	☐	☐

Discussion Strategy: Who doesn't appreciate being asked about their thoughts on a subject? By **asking for opinions and ideas**, you'll not only help others become involved in the discussion, but also enrich the discussion itself as a result. It's as easy as asking, "What do you think?" The next step—listening—is where your learning begins!

C. In small groups, discuss one or more of these topics. Try to use the discussion strategies you have learned.

- Did any ideas from the lecture seem new or especially interesting to you?
- Do you think an emergency response plan should be a spending priority?
- Does your government do a good job of protecting its people? In what ways?

REVIEW *your* notes

Work with a partner. Use your notes. If you have any question marks (?) in your notes, see if your partner can help you with the answers. You can ask yourself or your partner questions using the following phrases.

> I wonder why . . .
>
> I'd like to know . . .
>
> What does . . . mean?
>
> I wonder what caused . . .
>
> I wonder why (the speaker) concluded that . . .

Complete the notes below.

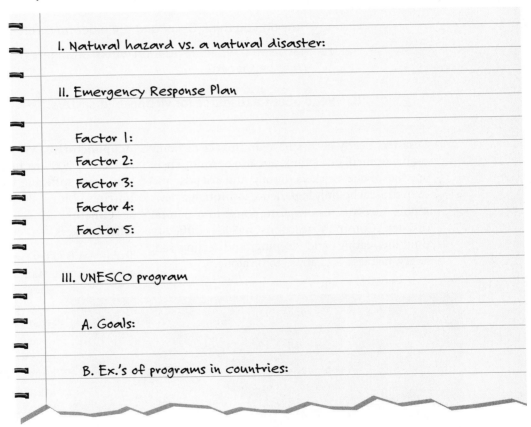

I. Natural hazard vs. a natural disaster:

II. Emergency Response Plan

    Factor 1:

    Factor 2:

    Factor 3:

    Factor 4:

    Factor 5:

III. UNESCO program

    A. Goals:

    B. Ex.'s of programs in countries:

Now you are ready to take the Unit Test.

TAKE THE UNIT TEST

Tip!

Mark places in your notes where you missed information or didn't understand something. This will remind you to follow up later.

EXTEND *the* topic

For every disaster, there's an opportunity to help. Listen to, read about, and research stories of people helping people in need after disaster strikes.

 A. Listen to a radio interview with a community emergency worker telling about three teenagers who saved a boy from a mudslide. Discuss these questions with your classmates.

1. How do you think Oscar and the older boys felt?

2. Have you been in a situation where strangers helped each other? What happened?

B. Read about a resource for victims of disasters.

Disasters nearly always have an impact not only on the immediate victims, but also beyond. There are the rescue workers, family and friends, and even those who only experience it through a news report. Stress is a normal response to a natural disaster. Common reactions include difficulty thinking, eating, and sleeping; and feeling sad, angry, helpless, and afraid to be alone.

Acupuncturists Without Borders (AWB) was started in 2005 to help people in New Orleans who were suffering from stress after Hurricane Katrina. More than eighty volunteers used acupuncture to treat victims and emergency relief workers.

Today AWB is trying to make community-wide acupuncture a standard part of the care offered after any disaster. Its mission has two parts: to provide stress treatment to communities after a disaster, and to teach local health-care workers techniques to reduce stress. AWB sees helping people manage stress as a vital step toward returning them to a normal life.

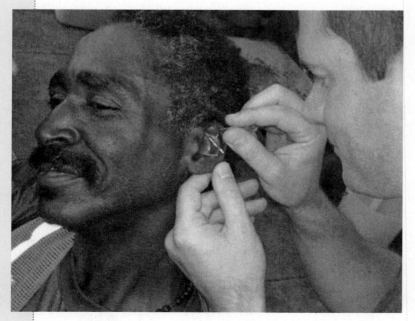

An acupuncturist treating a Hurricane Katrina victim

Work with a partner. Discuss the following questions.

1. What makes you nervous or stressed out? Name at least three things.

2. If we learn how to manage stress, in general, this will help us deal with emergencies. What do you do to relieve stress?

C. **Choose one of the following disaster projects to research. Prepare a short presentation.**

⟶ Interview someone who has survived a disaster, or go online using the keywords *disaster survivor stories* and find a story. Other options:
   • Search for Mieko "Miki" Browne, who survived a tsunami after floating away with her family inside their house.
   • Go to *www.childrenofphiphi.com* to see "The Children of Phi Phi Island," a collection of real-life stories written by Thai children about the tsunami that hit Phi Phi Island on December 26, 2004.
   • Visit *www.miamisci.org/hurricane/disasterquilt.html*—the Healing Quilt: a collection of survivor stories.

⟶ Find out about natural disaster relief organizations such as the International Federation of Red Cross and Red Crescent Societies. Go online and search for an example of a recent project anywhere in the world.

APPENDIX A: academic word list

Numbers indicate the sublist of the Academic Word List. For example, *abandon* and its family members are in Sublist 8. Sublist 1 contains the most frequent words in the list, and Sublist 10 contains the least frequent. **Boldfacing** indicates that the word is taught in *Contemporary Topic 2*. The page where the word can be found is indicated in parentheses beside the boldfaced word.

abandon	8	anticipate	9	bulk	9	**compile** (p. 93)	10
abstract	6	apparent	4	capable	6	complement	8
academy	5	append	8	capacity	5	complex	2
access (p. 103)	4	appreciate	8	category	2	**component** (p. 33)	3
accommodate	9	approach	1	cease	9	compound	5
accompany	8	appropriate	2	**challenge** (p. 63)	5	comprehensive	7
accumulate	8	approximate	4	channel	7	comprise	7
accurate (p. 43)	6	arbitrary	8	chapter	2	compute	2
achieve	2	area	1	chart	8	conceive	10
acknowledge (p. 13)	6	aspect	2	chemical	7	**concentrate** (p. 103)	4
acquire	2	assemble	10	circumstance	3	concept	1
adapt (p. 83)	7	**assess** (p. 43)	1	cite	6	conclude	2
adequate (p. 93)	4	**assign** (p. 3)	6	civil	4	concurrent	9
adjacent	10	assist	2	clarify	8	conduct	2
adjust	5	assume	1	**classic** (p. 3)	7	confer	4
administrate	2	assure	9	clause	5	confine	9
adult	7	attach	6	code	4	confirm	7
advocate	7	attain	9	coherent	9	**conflict** (p. 53)	5
affect	2	attitude	4	coincide	9	conform	8
aggregate	6	attribute	4	collapse	10	consent	3
aid	7	author	6	colleague	10	consequent	2
albeit	10	authority	1	commence	9	considerable	3
allocate (p. 113)	6	automate	8	comment	3	consist	1
alter (p. 53)	5	available	1	commission	2	**constant** (p. 23)	3
alternative	3	**aware** (p. 43)	5	commit	4	constitute	1
ambiguous	8	behalf	9	commodity	8	constrain	3
amend	5	benefit	1	**communicate** (p. 13)	4	construct	2
analogy	9	bias	8	community	2	consult	5
analyze	1	bond	6	compatible	9	consume	2
annual	4	brief	6	compensate	3	contact	5

contemporary	8	despite	4	ensure	3	fluctuate	8
context	1	detect	8	entity	5	focus	2
contract	1	deviate	8	environment	1	format	9
contradict	8	device	9	equate	2	formula	1
contrary	7	devote	9	equip	7	forthcoming	10
contrast (p. 33)	4	differentiate	7	equivalent	5	found	9
contribute (p. 33)	3	dimension	4	erode	9	**foundation** (p. 73)	7
controversy	9	diminish	9	error	4	framework	3
convene	3	discrete	5	establish	1	function	1
converse	9	**discriminate** (p. 3)	6	estate	6	fund	3
convert	7	displace	8	estimate	1	fundamental	5
convince	10	display	6	**ethic** (p. 93)	9	furthermore	6
cooperate (p. 113)	6	dispose	7	ethnic	4	**gender** (p. 3)	6
coordinate	3	distinct	2	evaluate	2	generate	5
core	3	distort	9	eventual	8	**generation** (p. 3)	5
corporate	3	distribute	1	evident	1	**globe** (p. 13)	7
correspond	3	diverse	6	evolve	5	goal	4
couple	7	document	3	exceed	6	grade	7
create	1	**domain** (p. 13)	6	exclude	3	grant	4
credit	2	domestic	4	exhibit	8	**guarantee** (p. 33)	7
criteria	3	dominate	3	expand	5	guideline	8
crucial (p. 83)	8	draft	5	expert	6	hence	4
culture	2	drama	8	explicit	6	hierarchy	7
currency	8	**duration** (p. 23)	9	exploit	8	highlight	8
cycle	4	**dynamic** (p. 73)	7	export	1	hypothesis	4
data	1	economy	1	**expose** (p. 83)	5	**identical** (p. 103)	7
debate	4	edit	6	external	5	identify	1
decade (p. 53)	7	element	2	**extract** (p. 103)	7	ideology	7
decline (p. 53)	5	eliminate	7	**facilitate** (p. 13)	5	**ignorance** (p. 113)	6
deduce	3	emerge	4	factor	1	illustrate	3
define	1	**emphasis** (p. 33)	3	feature	2	**image** (p. 3)	5
definite	7	empirical	7	federal	6	immigrate	3
demonstrate (p. 43)	3	enable	5	fee	6	impact	2
denote	8	encounter	10	file	7	implement	4
deny	7	energy	5	final	2	implicate	4
depress	10	enforce	5	finance	1	implicit	8
derive	1	**enhance** (p. 63)	6	finite	7	imply	3
design	2	enormous	10	flexible	6	impose	4

incentive	6	investigate	4	minimal	9	parallel	4
incidence (p. 83)	6	invoke	10	**minimize** (p. 113)	8	parameter	4
incline	10	involve	1	minimum	6	participate	2
income	1	isolate	7	ministry	6	partner	3
incorporate	6	issue	1	minor	3	passive	9
index	6	item	2	mode	7	perceive	2
indicate	1	job	4	modify	5	percent	1
individual	1	journal	2	monitor	5	period	1
induce	8	justify	3	motive	6	persist	10
inevitable	8	label	4	mutual	9	**perspective** (p. 33)	5
infer	7	labor	1	negate	3	phase	4
infrastructure	8	layer	3	**network** (p. 53)	5	phenomenon	7
inherent	9	lecture	6	neutral	6	philosophy	3
inhibit	6	legal	1	**nevertheless** (p. 13)	6	**physical** (p. 23)	3
initial	3	legislate	1	nonetheless	10	plus	8
initiate	6	levy	10	norm	9	policy	1
injure	2	liberal	5	normal	2	portion	9
innovate	7	license	5	**notion** (p. 43)	5	pose	10
input	6	likewise	10	notwithstanding	10	positive	2
insert	7	link	3	nuclear	8	potential	2
insight	9	locate	3	**objective** (pp. 73, 93)	5	practitioner	8
inspect	8	**logic** (p. 43)	5	obtain	2	**precede** (p. 13)	6
instance	3	maintain	2	obvious	4	precise	5
institute	2	major	1	occupy	4	**predict** (p. 113)	4
instruct	6	manipulate	8	occur	1	predominant	8
integral	9	manual	9	odd	10	preliminary	9
integrate	4	margin	5	offset	8	presume	6
integrity	10	mature	9	ongoing	10	previous	2
intelligence	6	maximize	3	**option** (p. 43)	4	primary	2
intense	8	mechanism	4	orient	5	**prime** (p. 3)	5
interact	3	media	7	outcome	3	principal	4
intermediate	9	mediate	9	output	4	**principle** (p. 73)	1
internal	4	**medical** (p. 103)	5	overall	4	prior	4
interpret	1	medium	9	overlap	9	**priority** (p. 113)	7
interval	6	**mental** (p. 43)	5	overseas	6	proceed	1
intervene	7	method	1	panel	10	process	1
intrinsic	10	migrate	6	**paradigm** (p. 93)	7	**professional** (p. 93)	4
invest	2	military	9	paragraph	8	prohibit	7

project (p. 63)	4	respond	1	stable	5	thesis	7
promote (p. 83)	4	restore	8	**statistic** (p. 103)	4	topic	7
proportion	3	restrain	9	status	4	trace	6
prospect	8	restrict	2	straightforward	10	tradition	2
protocol	9	**retain** (p. 13)	4	strategy	2	transfer	2
psychology (p. 23)	5	**reveal** (p. 103)	6	**stress** (pp. 73, 83)	4	transform	6
publication	7	revenue	5	structure	1	transit	5
publish	3	reverse	7	style	5	**transmit** (p. 83)	7
purchase	2	revise	8	submit	7	transport	6
pursue	5	revolution	9	subordinate	9	trend	5
qualitative	9	rigid	9	subsequent	4	trigger	9
quote	7	role	1	subsidy	6	**ultimate** (p. 113)	7
radical	8	route	9	substitute	5	undergo	10
random	8	scenario	9	successor	7	**underlie** (p. 94)	6
range	2	schedule	8	**sufficient** (p. 63)	3	undertake	4
ratio	5	scheme	3	sum	4	uniform	8
rational (p. 23)	6	scope	6	**summary** (p. 63)	4	unify	9
react	3	section	1	supplement	9	unique	7
recover (p. 83)	6	sector	1	survey	2	**utilize** (p. 73)	6
refine	9	secure	2	survive	7	valid	3
regime	4	seek	2	suspend	9	vary	1
region	2	select	2	sustain	5	vehicle	8
register	3	sequence	3	**symbol** (p. 3)	5	version	5
regulate	2	series	4	tape	6	via	8
reinforce	8	sex	3	**target** (p. 113)	5	violate	9
reject	5	shift	3	task	3	virtual	8
relax	9	significant	1	team	9	visible	7
release	7	similar	1	technical	3	vision	9
relevant	2	simulate	7	technique	3	visual	8
reluctance	10	site	2	technology	3	volume	3
rely	3	so-called	10	temporary	9	voluntary	7
remove	3	sole	7	tense	8	welfare	5
require	1	somewhat	7	terminate	8	whereas	5
research	1	source	1	text	2	whereby	10
reside	2	specific	1	theme	8	**widespread** (p. 113)	8
resolve (p. 63)	4	specify	3	theory	1		
resource	2	sphere	9	thereby	8		

APPENDIX B: affix charts

It is extremely important to have a strong vocabulary to succeed in university-level courses. One way to develop your vocabulary skills is to learn the affixes—prefixes and suffixes—that are commonly used in English. A prefix is a letter or group of letters at the beginning of a word. It usually changes the meaning. A suffix is a letter or group of letters at the end of a word. It usually changes the part of speech. Learning the meanings of affixes can help you identify unfamiliar words that you read or hear.

The charts below and on page 127 contain common prefixes and suffixes. Refer to the charts as you use this book.

PREFIX	MEANING	EXAMPLE
a-, ab-, il-, im-, in-, ir-, un-	not, without	atypical, abnormal illegal, impossible, inconvenient, irregular, unfair
anti-	opposed to, against	antisocial, antiseptic
co-, col-, com-, con-, cor-	with, together	coexist, collect, commune, connect, correct
de-	give something the opposite quality	decriminalize
dis-	not, remove	disapprove, disarm
ex-	no longer, former	ex-wife, ex-president
ex-	out, from	export, exit
extra-	outside, beyond	extracurricular, extraordinary
in-, im-	in, into	incoming, import
inter-	between, among	international
post-	later than, after	postgraduate
pro-	in favor of	pro-education
semi-	half, partly	semicircle, semi-literate
sub-	under, below, less important	subway, submarine, subordinate
super-	larger, greater, stronger	supermarket, supervisor

SUFFIX	MEANING	EXAMPLE
-able, -ible	having the quality of, capable of (adj)	comfortable, responsible
-al, -ial	relating to (adj)	professional, ceremonial
-ence, -ance, -ency, -ancy,	the act, state, or quality of (n)	performance, intelligence competency, conservancy
-ation, -tion, -ion	the act, state, or result of (n)	examination, selection, facilitation
-er, -or, -ar, -ist	someone who does a particular thing (n)	photographer, editor, beggar, psychologist
-ful	full of (adj)	beautiful, harmful, fearful
-ify, -ize	give something a particular quality (v)	clarify, modernize
-ility	the quality of (n)	affordability, responsibility, humility
-ism	a political or religious belief system (n)	atheism, capitalism
-ist	relating to (or someone who has) a political or religious belief (adj, n)	Buddhist, socialist
-ive, -ous, -ious,	having a particular quality (adj)	creative, dangerous, mysterious
-ity	a particular quality (n)	popularity, creativity
-less	without (adj)	careless, worthless
-ly	in a particular way (adj., adv.)	briefly, fluently
-ment	conditions that result from something (n)	government, development
-ness	quality of (n)	happiness, seriousness

CD: tracking guide

TRACK	ACTIVITY	PAGE
CD 1		
1	Introduction	
UNIT 1		
2	Build Your Vocabulary	3
3	Try It Out!	5
4	Listen for Main Ideas and Listen for Details	6–7
5	Talk About the Topic, Parts A and B	8
6	Take the Unit Test	9
7	Extend the Topic, Part A	10
UNIT 2		
8	Build Your Vocabulary	13
9	Try It Out!	15
10	Listen for Main Ideas and Listen for Details	16–17
11	Talk About the Topic, Parts A and B	18
12	Take the Unit Test	19
13	Extend the Topic, Part A	20
UNIT 3		
14	Build Your Vocabulary	23
15	Try It Out!	25
16	Listen for Main Ideas and Listen for Details	26–27
17	Talk About the Topic, Parts A and B	28
18	Take the Unit Test	29
19	Extend the Topic, Part A	30
UNIT 4		
20	Build Your Vocabulary	33
21	Try It Out!	35
22	Listen for Main Ideas and Listen for Details	36–37
23	Talk About the Topic, Parts A and B	38
24	Take the Unit Test	39
25	Extend the Topic, Part A	40

TRACK	ACTIVITY	PAGE
CD 2		
1	Introduction	
UNIT 5		
2	Build Your Vocabulary	43
3	Try It Out!	45
4	Listen for Main Ideas and Listen for Details	46–47
5	Talk About the Topic, Parts A and B	48
6	Take the Unit Test	49
7	Extend the Topic, Part A	50
UNIT 6		
8	Build Your Vocabulary	53
9	Try It Out!	55
10	Listen for Main Ideas and Listen for Details	56–57
11	Talk About the Topic, Parts A and B	58
12	Take the Unit Test	59
13	Extend the Topic, Part A	60
UNIT 7		
14	Build Your Vocabulary	63
15	Try It Out!	65
16	Listen for Main Ideas and Listen for Details	66–67
17	Talk About the Topic, Parts A and B	68
18	Take the Unit Test	69
19	Extend the Topic, Part A	70
UNIT 8		
20	Build Your Vocabulary	73
21	Try It Out!	75
22	Listen for Main Ideas and Listen for Details	76–77
23	Talk About the Topic, Parts A and B	78
24	Take the Unit Test	79
25	Extend the Topic, Part A	80

TRACK	ACTIVITY	PAGE
CD 3		
1	Introduction	
UNIT 9		
2	Build Your Vocabulary	83
3	Try It Out!	85
4	Listen for Main Ideas and Listen for Details	86–87
5	Talk About the Topic, Parts A and B	88
6	Take the Unit Test	89
7	Extend the Topic, Part A	90
UNIT 10		
8	Build Your Vocabulary	93
9	Try It Out!	95
10	Listen for Main Ideas and Listen for Details	96–97
11	Talk About the Topic, Parts A and B	98
12	Take the Unit Test	99
13	Extend the Topic, Part A	100
UNIT 11		
14	Build Your Vocabulary	103
15	Try It Out!	105
16	Listen for Main Ideas and Listen for Details	106–107
17	Talk About the Topic, Parts A and B	108
18	Take the Unit Test	109
19	Extend the Topic, Part A	110
UNIT 12		
20	Build Your Vocabulary	113
21	Try It Out!	115
22	Listen for Main Ideas and Listen for Details	116–117
23	Talk About the Topic, Parts A and B	118
24	Take the Unit Test	119
25	Extend the Topic, Part A	120

DVD: tracking guide

UNIT	FEATURE	STUDENT BOOK ACTIVITY

1	Lecture
	  Coaching Tips
	  Presentation Points
	Student Discussion
		Listen for Main Ideas and Listen for Details, pages 6–7
		
		Talk About the Topic, Parts A and B, page 8

2	Lecture
	  Coaching Tips
	  Presentation Points
	Student Discussion
		Listen for Main Ideas and Listen for Details, pages 16–17
		
		Talk About the Topic, Parts A and B, page 18

3	Lecture
	  Coaching Tips
	  Presentation Points
	Student Discussion
		Listen for Main Ideas and Listen for Details, pages 26–27
		
		Talk About the Topic, Parts A and B, page 28

4	Lecture
	  Coaching Tips
	  Presentation Points
	Student Discussion
		Listen for Main Ideas and Listen for Details, pages 36–37
		
		Talk About the Topic, Parts A and B, page 38

5	Lecture
	  Coaching Tips
	  Presentation Points
	Student Discussion
		Listen for Main Ideas and Listen for Details, pages 46–47
		
		Talk About the Topic, Parts A and B, page 48

6	Lecture
	  Coaching Tips
	  Presentation Points
	Student Discussion
		Listen for Main Ideas and Listen for Details, pages 56–57
		
		Talk About the Topic, Parts A and B, page 58

UNIT	FEATURE	STUDENT BOOK ACTIVITY

7	Lecture
	   Coaching Tips
	   Presentation Points
	Student Discussion
		Listen for Main Ideas and Listen for Details, pages 66–67
		
		Talk About the Topic, Parts A and B, page 68

8	Lecture
	   Coaching Tips
	   Presentation Points
	Student Discussion
		Listen for Main Ideas and Listen for Details, pages 76–77
		
		Talk About the Topic, Parts A and B, page 78

9	Lecture
	   Coaching Tips
	   Presentation Points
	Student Discussion
		Listen for Main Ideas and Listen for Details, pages 86–87
		
		Talk About the Topic, Parts A and B, page 88

10	Lecture
	   Coaching Tips
	   Presentation Points
	Student Discussion
		Listen for Main Ideas and Listen for Details, pages 96–97
		
		Talk About the Topic, Parts A and B, page 98

11	Lecture
	   Coaching Tips
	   Presentation Points
	Student Discussion
		Listen for Main Ideas and Listen for Details, pages 106–107
		
		Talk About the Topic, Parts A and B, page 108

12	Lecture
	   Coaching Tips
	   Presentation Points
	Student Discussion
		Listen for Main Ideas and Listen for Details, pages 116–117
		
		Talk About the Topic, Parts A and B, page 118

credits

Photo Credits: **Page 2** (left) Shutterstock, (center) © Tony Roberts/Corbis, (right) Shutterstock; **Page 6** Shutterstock; **Page 10** © Purestock/SuperStock; **Page 11** (left) Archive Photos, (right) © Bettman/Corbis; **Page 12** (left) Courtesy of the author, (center) Courtesy of the author, (right) Courtesy of the author, (bottom) Shutterstock; **Page 16** Photodisc/Corbis; **Page 20** Shutterstock; **Page 21** Digital Vision Ltd./SuperStock; **Page 22** (left) BananaStock/SuperStock, (right) Shutterstock; **Page 30** (left) Shutterstock, (center) Shutterstock, (right) Polka Dot Images/Jupiterimages; **Page 31** (left) Brand X/SuperStock, (right) Shutterstock; **Page 32** (left) BananaStock/SuperStock, (right) UpperCut Images/SuperStock; **Page 42** (left) Shutterstock, (right) Shutterstock; **Page 46** Will Faller; **Page 51** (left) Getty Images, (center) © Duomo/William R. Sallaz, Duomo Photography Ltd; **Page 52** Shutterstock; **Page 57** Shutterstock; **Page 60** Shutterstock; **Page 61** Shutterstock; **Page 62** Shutterstock; **Page 67** Shutterstock; **Page 70** Shutterstock **Page 71** © 2001 Photodisc; **Page 72** (left) Photodisc/SuperStock, (center) SuperStock, (right) Shutterstock; **Page 74** Shutterstock; **Page 80** Shutterstock; **Page 81** © Luke Cole 2003; **Page 82** Shutterstock; **Page 87** Shutterstock; **Page 91** © Neil Benvie/Corbis; **Page 92** (left) Shutterstock, (right) Shutterstock; **Page 97** Shutterstock; **Page 101** Ryan McVay/Getty Images; **Page 102** © Harley Schwadron/CartoonStock; **Page 110** National Geographic/Getty Images; **Page 111** © EyeWire, Inc.; **Page 112** (left) Courtesy of the author, (right) Shutterstock; **Page 120** Courtesy of the author; **Page 121** © James A. Sugar/Corbis

These are the **discussion strategies** that you will hear the students in the Student Discussion videos using. Consider starting a list of the expressions you learn for each one.

- Asking for opinions or ideas
- Expressing an opinion
- Agreeing
- Disagreeing
- Offering a fact or example

- Asking for clarification or confirmation
- Keeping the discussion on topic
- Paraphrasing
- Trying to reach a consensus